Writing a Winning Business Plan

Writing a Winning Business Plan

Revised and Updated Fifth Edition

Matthew Record

Viva Books

New Delhi | Mumbai | Chennai | Kolkata | Bengaluru | Hyderabad | Kochi | Guwahati

First Indian Edition 2010

VIVA BOOKS PRIVATE LIMITED

- 4737/23 Ansari Road, Daryaganj, New Delhi 110 002
  E-mail: vivadelhi@vivagroupindia.net, Tel. 42242200
- 76, Service Industries, Shirvane, Sector 1, Nerul, Navi Mumbai 400 706
  E-mail: vivamumbai@vivagroupindia.net, Tel. 27721273, 27721274
- Jamals Fazal Chambers, 26 Greams Road, Chennai 600 006
  E-mail: vivachennai@vivagroupindia.net, Tel. 28290304, 28294241
- B-103, Jindal Towers, 21/1A/3 Darga Road, Kolkata 700 017
  E-mail: vivakolkata@vivagroupindia.net, Tel. 22836381, 22816713
- 7, Sovereign Park Apartments, 56-58, K. R. Road, Basavanagudi, Bengaluru 560 004
  E-mail: vivabangalore@vivagroupindia.net, Tel. 26607409, 26607410
- 101-102 Mughal Marc Apartments, 3-4-637 to 641, Narayanguda, Hyderabad 500 029
  E-mail: vivahyderabad@vivagroupindia.net, Tel. 27564481, 27564482
- Beevi Towers, First Floor, SRM Road, Kaloor, Kochi 682 018, Kerala
  E-mail: vivakochi@vivagroupindia.net, Tel: 0484-2403055, 2403056
- 232, GNB Road, Beside UCO Bank, Silpukhuri, Guwahati 781 003
  E-mail: vivaguwahati@vivagroupindia.net, Tel: 0361-2666386

www.vivagroupindia.com

Published by arrangement with
How to Books
Spring Hill House, Spring Hill Road
Begbroke, Oxford OX5 1RX,
United Kingdom

NOTE: The material contained in this book is set out in good faith for general guidance and no liability can be accepted for loss or expense incurred as a result of relying in particular circumstances on statements made in the book. The laws and regulations are complex and liable to change, and readers should check the current position with the relevant authorited before making personal arrangements.

ISBN : 978-81-309-1459-6

Published by Vinod Vasishtha for Viva Books Private Limited, 4737/23, Ansari Road, New Delhi-110 002. Printed and bound by Swan Press, New Delhi.

M0000

Contents

List of Illustrations

Preface

Preparing a winning business plan is crucial to help ensure the success of your business. A well researched and carefully structured business plan is the single most important component in the development and continuation of any venture. It is a detailed map that shows where you're going and allows you to identify potential problems long before they arrive. With poor planning being the major cause of business failure, this book could literally save your business and your livelihood!

Whether you run an established business or are contemplating a new start-up venture, a business plan will convey your company's plans and illustrate how they can be achieved. You need it to measure performance, monitor progress, make future plans and raise additional finance.

This fifth edition has been thoroughly revised to provide you with up-to-date information and contact addresses should you need further advice. It is hoped that this book will help you on your way, though it must not be considered a substitute for taking detailed professional advice.

Matthew Record

1

Writing a Business Plan

The fact you have this book in your hands means that you are already aware of the importance of a business plan. With business failing at an alarming rate the need has never been greater to start off on the right foot with a clear understanding of exactly what you hope to achieve and how you will do it. A well thought out and carefully structured business plan is the key to the long-term success of any business. Whether you are just starting a business, buying one already established or perhaps in need of extra finance for expansion you will need a business plan.

UNDERSTANDING THE NEED FOR A BUSINESS PLAN

Reasons for a business plan

Your reason for compiling a plan will be different for each situation:

- If you are starting a new business you will require a plan to clearly assess every aspect of the business and show how it will succeed.
- If you are buying an already established business you will need to identify the strengths and weaknesses of the business to decide if you will be able to make it a success.
- If you are already up and running and in need of extra finance you will need a plan to convince those putting capital into your business that you can and will succeed.
- If you are applying for one of the many grants available.

Who will read your plan?

When you begin to compile a business plan you must always remember who the plan is for. Just as an author must always remember who will read his books so you must remember who will read your business plan. With this in mind you must present your plan in a clear and logical format. This will enable the recipient to achieve a clear understanding of your business and make a decision based on the information you have supplied.

Your business plan will benefit the various types of people who will all be using your plan as a basis for making decisions:

- your bank manager;
- alternative providers of finance;
- business advisory organisations;
- friends and colleagues who will invest in your business;
- yourself and your work colleagues who will be running the business and using the plan on a daily basis.

ASSESSING YOURSELF

Launching a new business or buying an existing one is a huge step that shouldn't be taken lightly. However with the right forethought and careful planning the transition from being a salaried employee to a self-employed worker should be a simple process. But before you take the plunge and tell your boss what he can do with his job, make sure you have the abilities needed to run your own business and that you have chosen a business that will suit your abilities. It is no good considering setting up a business to repair DVD recorders if your only experience of them is to press a few buttons to record your favourite programme.

Self-motivation

You must find your business both stimulating and exciting to run, or you will find yourself getting bored and your enthusiasm draining. It does not matter if your friends find your particular business idea uninteresting; it is what makes *you* satisfied that counts. After all it is you who will be investing time, energy and money in your business, not your friends.

Have you got what it takes?

The dream of owning your own business and becoming your own boss will for many remain just that, a dream. However, for those with the determination and drive to turn their dreams into reality, then anything is possible. As you are reading this book it is assumed you are one of this number ready to take your future into your hands and become your own boss.

Becoming committed

In the early days your business will demand your total commitment for very little financial reward. This can put a great strain on both yourself and your family so sacrifices will have to be made. You will probably have to survive on a reduced income whilst the business is getting established. The annual holiday in the sun will be postponed for a while and very few evenings and weekends will be totally free from work. You and your family must believe in your business and be prepared to adapt to the inevitable changes to your lifestyle that a new business brings with it.

Learning to be in charge

All the hard work associated with starting your own business should be outweighed by the many benefits being your own boss will bring. You will no longer be taking orders from someone else, it is you who will be giving them. No longer are you just another number or a face within a workforce, you are the person at the top, the one who makes all the decisions and ultimately it's you who will be responsible for the success of your business.

You will have to remember though, it is you who will have to put things right when they go wrong, it is you who will have to stand behind your decisions and it is you whom people will turn to for advice and support. If you are ready to accept these challenges with determination and enthusiasm then you are ready to accept the challenge of running your own business.

Ten key questions to ask yourself

Ask yourself these questions to see if you have what it takes to run your own business:

1. Are you hard working and determined to make a success of your new business?
2. Are you totally committed to becoming your own boss?
3. Are you a highly self motivated person who thrives on pressure and new challenges?
4. Can you organise yourself and your business to work efficiently, productively and profitably?
5. Are you prepared for setbacks and ready to accept that things will not always go as planned?
6. Can you make sound decisions and stick by them whatever the consequences?
7. Are you able to learn from your mistakes and ensure they never happen again?
8. Do you have previous experience of your chosen business idea?
9. Have you examined your potential market to ensure you are able to succeed in it?
10. Are your family and friends totally behind you and prepared to make sacrifices?

If you have been able to answer all of these questions with a positive and confident *YES* then you are well on the way to starting your own business and becoming your own boss.

CHOOSING YOUR BUSINESS

Once you have decided you have the necessary qualities and abilities to run your own business you must next decide on which business idea is right for you. There are many ways to become your own boss, these include:

- Discovering a new **niche** market and developing a product or service to fill it.

- Developing a product or service of **superior quality** to that of the competition and then competing with them.
- Buying an already **established business**, perhaps with unrealised potential.
- Buying a **franchise** opportunity and using an already proven successful business formula.
- Using the internet to set up an online business.

Whichever method of becoming your own boss you choose it will cost you time, money and energy to get up and running so you will have to make sure you are able to make a success of it.

GATHERING YOUR INFORMATION

It is at this stage you should start to gather information. If you need to write to a government department for help or advice, then do so now. Many organisations, particularly government bodies, are notorious for taking weeks or months to respond to an enquiry. There is nothing more annoying than sitting down to write up a section of your plan only to discover the information you need is not to hand.

The golden rule of information gathering is to collect as much of it as you possibly can. You can *never* have too much information.

Even something which doesn't seem to be important now may turn out to be crucial to your business plan at a later date.

COMPILING YOUR BUSINESS PLAN

Just as a book is separated into chapters which follow a logical sequence, so too should be your business plan. Here is an example of the section headings you could use to compile your plan:

Contents Page
The Executive Summary
The Nature of Your Business
Your Product or Service
Your Market and Competitors
Your Marketing Plan
Operations
Financial Forecasts
Financial Analysis
Appendices

A quick overview

Here is an overview; each heading is explained in detail later in the book:

Contents page

It is a matter of personal preference whether this follows or precedes your executive summary.

The executive summary

This is a brief yet concise statement which is designed to give your reader an overview about your business by summarising the key points. Here you should describe the following:

- The current position of your business.
- Details about who will be buying your products or services, in what quantities and why.
- Your short-, medium- and long-term objectives and how they will be achieved.
- A summary of your financial forecasts.
- Details of how much money you need.

The nature of your business

This section of your plan should give your reader an understanding about who you are, what you do and how you do it. The following points should be covered:

- Your business name, address and contact telephone number.
- The legal status you will trade under.
- Details of your key members of staff including yourself.
- Your location.
- Your business objectives and how these will be achieved.
- Your mission statement.

Your market and competitors

This section of your business plan should describe the market you are in. It should highlight who your clients will be, what they will expect from your products or services, and details of who and where your competitors are.

Your marketing plan

Your marketing plan will describe how you will promote and sell your products or services. It will include details of:

- market research;
- your target market;
- the competition;
- marketing methods.

Operations

Your operational plan is the nuts and bolts of your business. It will illustrate to your reader the steps you will take to make sure your business will operate both successfully and profitably.

Financial forecasts

This is the most difficult part of compiling a business plan. Obviously you will feel optimistic, but it is essential to be realistic. Any bank manager who knows his job will be able to see through any proposal based on inflated figures which make the balance sheet look good. The only person you will be fooling is yourself. Your market research will be able to provide you with an accurate sales forecast.

Financial analysis

This will go hand in hand with the sales forecast as the sales forecast is presented in the form of cash flow forecasts which in turn lead to profit and loss and balance sheet forecasts.

Appendices

In the appendices you should include any information which will support and verify any statements and assumptions you have made in other areas of your business plan.

DESIGNING YOUR PLAN

There is no set formula for designing a successful business plan. Every plan will differ in length and style depending on the type of business. However there are characteristics which should be apparent in each of them.

Deciding the length

The length of your business plan will vary depending on the nature of the business. As a guideline your plan should be between 25 and 40 pages including the title pages and any appendices. Obviously if you have just invented a new car that runs on fresh air you are going to need a far more detailed document than if you are planning to set up a simple grass-cutting business.

The amount of capital you need to raise will also have an effect on the length of your plan. Generally speaking, the more capital you need, the longer the plan. If you are looking to raise £100,000 then anything less than 25 pages is unlikely to convince your bank manager to lend you money. However, if you only require a few hundred pounds, then a 40-page document is likely to bore the reader and overstate your case.

Choosing the right style

You will develop your own style of writing but you must always retain the interest of the reader and write in a narrative style using everyday terms. There is little point in using technical jargon if the reader cannot understand what you are trying to say. For example if 'it has a 456 micro buffer enhanced with a 789 extended memory data translator' means it is a fast and powerful machine, then just say it is a fast and powerful machine. Each sentence should follow on from the last in a logical sequence as should each chapter and sub-heading. Avoid trying to convey too many ideas in one sentence. Remember you are trying to make your business plan easy to read and understand.

SIMPLIFYING YOUR PLAN

The task of producing a business plan can seem daunting but with a little forethought you can turn it into a highly enjoyable experience, and this after all is one of the fundamental reasons for being in business – to have fun and enjoy what you are doing.

Ten steps to help you

1. Decide which business best suits you and where it should be located; remember to consider using the internet.

2. Compile market research data to summarise the competition.

3. Decide how much capital you are able to invest and then set your business objectives.

4. Decide on the legal structure of your business. Identify your target market.

5. Compile your marketing strategy to show how you will sell your product or service.

6. Work out how many employees you will need and what they will cost.

7. List any equipment you need and how much it will cost.

8. Compile your cash flow, profit and loss and balance sheet forecasts.
9. List your assumptions indicating how you arrived at these figures.
10. Write notes about each of the above points.

When you have completed all of these points you will be ready to start writing your business plan. Whatever the size of your business organisation you should be able to condense all the information you have gathered and wish to convey in 20 to 40 pages including all title pages. No one reading your plan will have the time to wade through a document the length of *War and Peace*.

EDITING YOUR PLAN

After you have gathered all your information the task of actually sitting down and writing your plan begins. The key to successful writing is to always compile a rough draft first then leave it for a few days. When you return to your draft, read it and then read it again, deciding how it can be improved. Only editing, re-writing and fine tuning will make your plan into the best document you can possibly produce. If possible, get a friend or colleague to read through your rough draft before you start on your master copy. Sometimes someone else's viewpoint can prove to be invaluable; there is no substitute for constructive criticism.

Preparing the master copy

When you begin compiling your master copy from your rough draft, take particular care that your document is grammatically correct and that any spelling mistakes have been corrected. If you are using a word processor to produce your plan, then do not just rely on the spell check facility to amend any spelling mistakes: some words with just a letter added or removed can make a different word which although spelt correctly is not grammatically correct.

Finding someone to read it

Before submitting your plan to anyone, get a friend or colleague to read through it and ask them if they understand what you are trying to convey. If there is any part of your plan they do not understand, then edit, re-write and fine tune until it does make sense. If they had a problem understanding it then you can be sure your intended business reader will have the same problem. Ultimately you are responsible for any errors, so make sure none remains.

Alternative methods for producing your business plan

In addition to compiling your business plan yourself there are a number of other options you could consider using:

- An accountant or business consultancy would be able to produce a business plan on your behalf, but the cost of this is likely to be quite considerable.
- There are a number of computer packages which are beneficial providing that you have completed the initial research yourself, these include:

  PlanIT Business Plan Deluxe – available from A World of Software, The Harlequin Centre, Watford WD17 2BU. Tel: 01923 630259. Email: orders@aworldofsoftware.com Website: www.aworldofsoftware.com

  Business Planner – available from Rosetta IT Solutions Limited. Tel: 01942 814814. Email: support@rosetta-it.com Website: www.rosetta-it.com

  Business Plan Pro – available from PaloAlto Software Limited, 72 Hammersmith Road, London W14 8TH. Tel: 0845 351 9924. Fax: 020 7900 2773. Email: sales@paloalto.co.uk Websites: www.businessplanpro.co.uk or www.paltalto.co.uk

  We are delighted to offer our readers a special 20% discount on Business Plan Pro (RRP £79.99) and Business Plan Pro Premier (RRP £129.99). To order please call 0845 351 9924 and mention this offer. For more information visit www.paloalto.co.uk or www.bplans.co.uk where you will find extensive free business planning resources that have been compiled by PaloAlto.

CHECKLIST

- Before you begin to compile your business plan, make absolutely sure you understand why a plan is necessary, who will be reading it and for what reasons.

- Take some time to really assess whether you have got what it takes to run the intended business. Being your own boss may sound very glamorous but are you ready to run your business professionally, competently and profitably?
- When you choose a business, be sure to choose the right one and enjoy what you are doing.
- Research your intended new business or business opportunity fully. Look into every aspect and detail of the set up and operation to make sure you know what to expect.
- With all the necessary information to hand begin to compile a rough draft of your business plan, paying particular attention to detail and to the design, layout and keeping a simple appearance.
- When you compile your finished plan from your rough draft, pay particular attention to editing and eliminate all spelling, grammar and punctuation mistakes.

Case Studies

Joshua and Jake want to buy a franchise

Joshua and Jake are two friends who have worked together in a retail store for the past six years. They have developed an excellent working relationship and are also good friends away from their working environment. An opportunity to buy an established franchise business close to their homes has been advertised in a local newspaper. The present proprietor wishes to retire due to ill health and has reluctantly put the business up for sale. Following a meeting with both the franchise company and the proprietor, Joshua and Jake decide they want to buy the business and run it between themselves.

Jasmine discovers a market niche

Jasmine has spent the last three years working in a greetings card shop. During that time she has discovered a new niche market to produce personalised calendars and diaries with all of her clients' important dates already printed out. Calendar Creations will be financed from her own savings but she will be compiling a business plan to put her business objectives into context. This will let her know if she has a viable business concept or just a pipe dream.

Luke looks to expand

Luke runs his own engineering company and currently employs 30 people who help him generate a £2 million turnover. His company has just won a large contract to supply a large car manufacturer with various components and equipment. The contract would involve employing extra staff, to cope with the demand, and expanding his existing premises on either his existing site or relocating to larger premises perhaps even in a new area. Luke is looking to finance the expansion with a combination of investments and grants. He needs a business plan to convince both potential investors that he has a business worth investing in and the various government departments that he would be eligible for grant assistance.

2

Your Business Idea

In order to effectively convey your business idea to others it is essential to define clearly the basic structure of your business. Your business idea forms the nucleus of your business plan and is the starting point from which every other aspect will emanate. A clear definition of your intentions is essential for investors to make informed decisions regarding your proposal.

This chapter will cover the processes involved in setting up your business. All the sections are equally important and will form the introductory part of your business plan. From this information the reader must be able to gain a clear and concise understanding of your business idea.

PLANNING YOUR LEGAL ENTITY

Once you have decided which type of business you would like to run the next task is to choose the legal entity you will trade under. There are three main types, each with its own set of advantages and disadvantages. We will look at each in more detail to help you decide which best suits your needs:

- sole trader;
- partnership;
- limited company;
- limited liability partnership (LLP).

Becoming a sole trader

As the name suggests this is usually a one-person business where one individual has been solely responsible for starting it up and raising all the necessary capital.

There is very little red tape with this type of business and there are no particular legal formalities to adhere to. However, within the first three months of trading you must register as self-employed with HM Revenue & Customs (HMRC) or you may have to pay a £100 penalty. A self-employed registration form (CWF1) can be downloaded from the HM Revenue & Customs website at www.hmrc.gov.uk/selfemployed. You will also need to pay fixed rate Class 2 National Insurance contributions (NICs) and Class 4 NICs on your profits which will be taxed as income. In addition, if your business has, or expects to have, a turnover in excess of £64,000 per annum then you also need to apply for a Value Added Tax (VAT) number. This means that you must charge VAT on your sales, complete a VAT return and send your VAT payments to HM Revenue & Customs. Further help and advice can be obtained from HMRC but depending on your precise enquiry, a number of different contact points are available. To find out which department to contact either consult your local telephone directory or visit search2.hmrc.gov.uk/kbroker/hmrc/contactus/start.jsp

Going into partnership

A partnership is similar to a sole trader in that it is relatively simple to establish. Each partner must register as self-employed and submit an annual self-assessment return to HMRC. All partners have unlimited liability for all partnership debts and must keep accurate records showing business income and expenditure, which also need to be submitted to HMRC. Partnerships may comprise anything from two to 20 members, each with the same objective – to make a profit. For this reason a charity cannot become a partnership.

As with a sole trader, a partnership does not have to be registered and it is not compulsory to have any form of partnership agreement. However it is strongly advisable to have such an agreement drawn up by a solicitor at the outset of your business, even if your business partner is your wife, husband or best friend. That way, if there is ever any dispute, both parties will have a document to refer to. It would cover such things as:

1. How will decisions be reached if the partners disagree?
2. How much money will each partner put in?
3. What will happen if one partner wants to pull out?

You may wish to include a sleeping partner in the business. A sleeping partner would provide capital but have no say in the day-to-day running of the business. The sleeping partner may choose to become a limited partner which means they would only be liable for their initial investment and nothing else. At least one member of a partnership must be a general partner with unlimited liability for all the debts of the partnership. A partnership, like a sole trader, is not legally bound to publish its accounts.

Setting up a limited liability partnership (LLP)

LLPs are similar to ordinary partnerships in that risks, costs, debts, responsibilities and profits are shared between members, who can be individuals or limited companies. However, the liability of members is limited to the amount of money they have invested or personally guaranteed when raising finance. LLPs must register at Companies House and at least two members must be *designated members* who have additional legal responsibilities placed upon them. Further information about these responsibilities can be obtained from Companies House.

LLPs are required to file annual accounts with Companies House and each member must also submit an annual self-assessment return to HMRC. Members are taxed on their share of the profits and pay National Insurance contributions (NICs), according to the structure of the business. For example, individuals pay income tax and NICs and limited company members will pay corporation tax.

Forming a limited company

Limited companies are the most complex type of business to set up. Once formed, a limited company is a legal entity quite separate from its owner(s). The individuals who own it are only financially responsible for paying for the shares they are issued with. A limited company has to pay corporation tax on its profits, and PAYE plus National Insurance contributions on behalf of its employees. If you are a director you will be treated as an employee and have Class 1 National Insurance and income tax deducted from your salary.

There are two types of limited company, private and public, each carrying advantages and disadvantages.

Further information about limited companies can be obtained by contacting Companies House at Crown Way, Maindy, Cardiff CF14 3UZ or by telephoning the Contact Centre on 0870 33 33 636. Alternatively, visit their website at www.companieshouse.gov.uk

Getting further help

There may be tax advantages to trading under a particular structure. For example, in the early years of a business when the profits may be small, it may be worth operating as a sole trader or partnership, and then registering as a limited company at a later date. Your accountant will be able to advise which is the best legal structure to suit your needs.

Make sure the accountant you choose is professionally qualified (which usually means 'chartered') and has a proven track record. Personal recommendation is the best way to find a good accountant. The financial penalties for poor advice could be severe. Good accountants should earn their fees from the money they save you in tax. The Institute of Chartered Accountants in England and Wales will be able to provide you with a list of its local members; it can be contacted at Moorgate Place, London EC2P 2BJ. Tel: 020 7920 8404. Website: www.icaew.com

CHOOSING YOUR TRADING NAME

Long and careful consideration should be given to your business trading name. It should reflect the image you wish to portray to your clients about who you are and what you do. For example, builders Dave Bodgitt and John Leggit would have more commercial success calling their partnership Dave and John's Building Services than simply Bodgitt and Leggit. You may feel the word Limited after your name will portray an image of a large organisation even if you are only a two-person team. Choosing a name begins to create an identity for your business.

Using a logo

The name you finally decide upon will appear on all your letterheads, compliment slips, business cards, invoices, order forms, vehicles and clothing to name but a few areas. Therefore it may be a good plan to incorporate a **logo** either within your trading name or as a separate graphic image. There are many advertising and marketing companies who will be able to design a logo for you. Be careful to agree on a written price before any work begins. If you do not, then the cost can be very high especially when the company starts to charge you for its 'thinking time'.

For a nominal charge most high street printers will produce a small selection of possible logos for you to choose from. You may have designed a logo yourself in which case it will be worth contacting **The Trade Marks Registry** who will be able to offer help and advice about applying for a trade mark. They can be contacted at Concept House, Cardiff Road, Newport, South Wales NP10 8QQ. Tel: 01633 811407.

Sensitive words and expressions

There are some words and expressions that you are not allowed to use within your business name without first getting official permission. These include words that suggest your business:

- is of national importance (British, Irish, Welsh, Scottish, English, National, International, European);
- has a special status (Association, Authority, Chamber of Commerce, Chartered Council, Institute, Society);
- performs a special function (Charity, Insurance, Register, Trust);
- performs a specialised activity (Architect, Chemist, Health Centre);
- has connections with Government or royalty (Parliament, Government, Royal, Queen, Prince).

This is to stop businesses claiming to be something that they are not. For further information see the *Company Names – BGF2* booklet, which is available to view or download from the Companies House website (www.companies house.gov.uk) or by telephoning the Companies House Contact Centre on 0870 33 33 636.

DEFINING THE NATURE OF YOUR BUSINESS

In order for the reader of your business plan to make any decision about the future of your business, you must first ensure that they know all there is to know about how your business works and why you believe your business will be successful. This section of your business plan will give you the opportunity to introduce the reader to your business idea by clearly summarising the nature of your business.

This will be an *overview* of how your business works; many of the topics will appear in greater detail later in your business plan. Be clear and precise in this overview but do not assume your reader will fully understand what you are trying to convey.

Including background information

It is a good idea to begin this section by giving the reader some background information about your business. Start by describing how you arrived at your business idea; state what your business name is and explain why you have chosen it. It is often said that when an investor puts capital into a business, they are not really backing 'the business' but the person behind the business. Therefore you must also describe the skills and experience you have which may be relevant to your business. This need only be an overview as your skills and experience will be covered later in this chapter under *Listing your key personnel* (page 24).

Giving trading details

The recipient will expect to know which legal form you will be trading under and why you have chosen it. If you have not yet started to trade then you can include the date you intend to start your business. Perhaps you intend to buy a business which is already established and trading, in which case the reader will want to know why the business is for sale and whether the asking price is fair. A personal recommendation from your accountant to substantiate the selling price will go a long way to convince the reader that you have got a good deal.

For an already established business state when, where and why the business was launched. Include a brief summary of the business's financial results and achievements to date. Copies of the actual annual accounts from previous years should be included in your appendix.

Describing Your Products or Services

When you write about your products or services, imagine your reader as a novice with little or no understanding of your business concept. It is very tempting to assume your reader will automatically understand what you are trying to convey, but by the end your reader must have more than a passing understanding of your products or services.

Obviously the more complex your product or service is, then the more detail you will have to go into. For example, if you have just developed a new method for converting sea water into drinking water at a fraction of the cost and time taken by the present desalination process, then you will have to explain in greater detail than if you are just about to start up a window cleaning business.

Avoid trying to 'sell' your products or services to your reader at this stage; that will come later when you meet face to face. Stick to the facts and be specific.

Protecting Your Business Idea

If you have developed a new product or invention – or indeed if your business idea is a totally new concept – then you should give serious thought to protecting intellectual property rights of your product, invention or idea against theft. This can be done in a number of ways depending on the nature of your business. There are four main types of protection, each one relating to a different aspect of your business.

- A **patent** protects how your product works.
- **Design registration** protects how your product looks.
- A **trade mark** protects what your product is called.
- A **copyright** protects your work on record, paper or film.

Further information about registering and protecting your intellectual property rights can be obtained from the UK Intellectual Property Office (IPO), which is the operating name of the Patent Office. The IPO is the official government body responsible for granting intellectual property rights in the United Kingdom, they can be contacted at Concept House, Cardiff Road, Newport NP10 8QQ. Tel: 0845 9500505 (Central Enquiries). Email: enquiries@ipo.gov.uk Website: www.ipo.gov.uk

Other useful addresses

The Chartered Institute of Patent Attorneys, 95 Chancery Lane, London WC2A 1DT. Tel: 020 7405 9450. Fax: 020 7430 0471. Email: mail@cipa.org.uk Website: www.cipa.org.uk

The Institute of Patentees and Inventors, PO Box 39296, London SE3 7WH. Tel: 0871 226 2091. Fax: 020 8293 5920. Email: ipi@invent.org.uk Website: www.invent.org.uk

Institute of Trade Mark Attorneys, Canterbury House, 2–6 Sydenham Road, Croydon, Surrey CR0 9XE. Tel: 020 8686 2052. Fax: 020 8680 5723. Email: tm@itma.org.uk Website: itma.org.uk

DEFINING YOUR BUSINESS OBJECTIVES

Now that the reader has a better understanding of your business concept, you are able to show them exactly what direction your business is going to take and how it will get there. Your business objectives will be a blueprint for you to work to which will show you what you hope to achieve and by when. It is very important to define your objectives clearly at the outset of your business; this will not only show the reader that you have thought through the long-term future of your business, but it will also put your ideas into context.

Everybody in business has a different set of objectives depending on who they are and the nature of their business. Your objectives may be as simple as to still be trading at the end of the first year, or as detailed as to obtain a 25 per cent market share by the end of your third year. Whatever your objectives are, be ready to substantiate any statements you make with facts and figures. Obviously you want to be optimistic but wild assumptions will cut no ice with your investors. Be as prudent as you possibly can; keep your objectives realistic and within reach. Remember, it is far better to under-estimate and over-achieve than to over-estimate and under-achieve.

Defining your short-term objectives

In general 'short term' means the initial twelve months of trading. If you have carefully thought about your objectives then you should be able to list them accurately and in the order they will be reached. As very few businesses make much profit in the first year, your short-term objective may be to survive the first year with a small overdraft and a full order book.

Defining your medium-term objectives

The medium term will cover the first two years. Obviously these will not be stated in as much detail as your short-term objectives but nevertheless they should still represent carefully calculated assumptions. Perhaps you would like to pay off your business loan or reduce your overdraft; if so your cashflow forecast should illustrate how.

Defining your long-term objectives

These objectives refer to the first three years and beyond and as such can be as broad as they are long. It is very difficult for anyone to estimate where a business will be after three years, so your long-term objectives can be stated in more general terms.

Your long-term objectives may include employing more staff, introducing more products or expanding your business. Whatever they are, they can be little more than dreams at this stage but they should still be sensible and achievable.

COMPILING YOUR MISSION STATEMENT

A mission statement is a brief definition of your overall business philosophy in relation to your products or services, and the level of client satisfaction that you wish to develop and maintain. Although only a brief statement it should encapsulate all of your business objectives and provide your staff, clients and yourself with a clear set of goals to work to.

Key points to make

Many large corporations will pay a small fortune to have their mission statement professionally compiled, but as long as you include the following points in your statement, then yours can be just as dynamic as theirs. State:

- what business you are in and why;
- your strategic goal, detailing what you want to achieve over the next one to three years;
- how you will do it, for example by quality of service or adhering to strict values and standards.

Over time your mission statement will have to change as your goals are met. If you achieve your intended goal to become the market leader then your statement will have to be updated to reflect this.

Example

> Phoenix Business Plans has been founded to fill a niche that exists in the market place. We will specialise in compiling professionally packaged business and marketing plans both rapidly and efficiently, at a fraction of our competitors' prices, whilst maintaining the highest levels of quality and client service at all times. It is our intention to become the market leader within the next five years. The success of our business will be directly influenced by our dedication to continually improve the quality and service in every aspect of our operation.

DESCRIBING YOUR LOCATION

Next in importance to the nature of your business is its location. In an ideal world every business would be located where it could achieve maximum profits for minimum cost, but as we do not live in such a world then your location must be chosen with the utmost care. If you work from home then your location is already defined. If not, the task of finding the perfect location can be very difficult.

The nature of your business will have a great bearing on your location. For example if you run a garage, restaurant or a shop, your clients will come to you and your location will be of paramount importance. If, however, you are in the construction, plumbing or electrical industry then you will have to go to your clients and your marketing skills will matter much more than your physical location.

If you are setting up an online business, then the same location principles apply whether you are running an online store or offering a local service. For example, the client base for an online store may include national and international customers so you will need to demonstrate how your physical location will not restrict sales. This can be achieved by highlighting how your distribution methods will service your customers irrespective of location.

LISTING YOUR KEY PERSONNEL

This section of your business plan will give you the opportunity to introduce the driving force of your business to the reader. By now the reader will have a very good understanding of what your business is all about, what you will be selling and how you will be selling it.

- Now is the time to show that you and your colleagues can make it happen.

Even if you have the simplest business concept ever, without the right mix of people behind you, your business will quickly stagnate.

Your potential investors are going to examine not only your business concept, but also your personal attributes. They will want to know, have you got what it takes to achieve long-term success? Are you prepared to work very long hours week in week out, even year in year out, with little reward to begin with? If you have any relevant skills, experience or qualifications, include them now. These can be evidenced by including your curriculum vitae and any certificates or diplomas in the appendix.

Show how you will make an excellent employer. Summarise your hiring strategy and any special features you will offer as an employer such as profit sharing, incentives for good work and flexible working hours.

For key staff members you should briefly describe their background including their name, previous relevant experience and success, educational and professional qualifications and details of their managerial methods.

CHECKLIST

- Have you decided which legal entity your business will trade under?
- Have you chosen the trading name you will use for your business?
- Have you explained the nature of your business?
- Have you described what you are selling to your reader in easy-to-understand terms?
- Is your reader aware of the aspirations you have for your business and what steps you will take to ensure that these are met?
- Is the mission statement you have compiled truly representative of what you want to achieve?
- Are the key members of your personnel described in such a way to highlight how they will contribute to the success of your business?

CASE STUDIES

Joshua and Jake approach the bank

The £25,000 asking price for the business has been pre-set by the franchise head office with little room for negotiation. However, after examining the previous three years' accounts, Joshua and Jake felt this appeared to be a fair price based on the present level of sales and overheads. They could raise £7,000 between themselves and an additional £3,000 from Joshua's parents. Their next task would be to approach the bank for the additional £15,000. Jake had held an account with a local bank for a number of years so it was decided to approach this bank first. A visit to the bank revealed the need to compile a business plan and for an appointment to then be made.

Jasmine conducts her own market research

Before Jasmine exchanges the security of a regular job and regular wages for the uncertainty of running her own business she decides to carry out her own market research study. She wants to see if she has a viable business concept. Working in a greetings card shop gives her an ideal opportunity to talk to people who are already buying calendars. The initial response is very encouraging, and Jasmine decides to go ahead with her own market research survey. High street shoppers are surveyed at various times of the day and week in order to obtain a good cross section of respondents. Once again Jasmine manages to generate a positive response.

Luke assesses his situation

Having been in business for five years gives Luke an edge when it comes to assessing his current situation and compiling a business plan. His financial forecast could be made with a certain degree of accuracy as most of his calculations would be based on recent experience. In order to cope with the extra workload which would be generated from his new contract, a £350,000 investment would be needed to bring his present premises up to date, and he would need a further £150,000 to buy new machinery.

Action points

1. List the main advantages and disadvantages of the various legal trading entities available to you. What are the benefits of choosing the entity you have?
2. Define your key business objectives? How will you ensure that these objectives are met?
3. Draw up a list of the ten main features and benefits of your product or service. Consider how these will make your clients buy from you.

3

Defining Your Market

Marketing means many different things to many different people. To some, marketing is merely a process that only large businesses should be concerned about; to others it is just an expensive way to find out what the client wants. Whatever your views on marketing are, you cannot hide from the fact that it is a necessity for each and every business no matter how big or small and not just an accessory for the larger businesses with huge budgets to spend. Marketing can be simply described as: how to bring in the business.

WHY USE MARKETING?

In the first instance you have to tell your clients about the product or service you are selling but more importantly you must be selling something that they actually want and will buy. This is where your marketing methods will prove to be invaluable. Marketing methods come in many shapes and sizes but can easily be summed up in one word, research. Your marketing methods will help you to identify your potential market and everything associated with it.

To just find out if your product or service will sell is not enough on its own. You need to be aware of:

- who will buy from you;
- how often will they buy;
- the amount they will buy;
- what they are prepared to pay;
- what they expect to get for their money;

- which newspapers they read;
- where to advertise to maximise the response;
- who and where your competitors are.

RESEARCHING YOUR CLIENTS

Your potential clients are one of the most important elements of your business. Without clients your business is nothing: it will cease to be. Treat your clients well and they will come back time after time, but upset them once and you may have lost them for life. Many new businesses are formed in the belief that as soon as they begin to trade then the clients will come. In reality nothing could be further from the truth.

Compiling a business plan is all about forward planning, and getting strategies to ensure that your business is both viable and profitable. Therefore, to even begin to consider the direction your business will take without first considering your client base is marketing suicide. Knowing and understanding who your clients are will be crucial when you are devising your marketing plan and deciding whom to target for your advertising and promotion. A truly successful business will provide a product or service which has a universal appeal to each and every client and is able to satisfy all of their needs.

SEGMENTING YOUR MARKET

The buzz words in marketing over the last few years have been 'market segmentation'. It is unlikely that your business will be able to sell to every part of the industry you are in. Instead you need to discover which segment of the market will be more lucrative and profitable.

Example: two restaurants

Two restaurants on opposite sides of the road may be in the same overall market of providing food for clients, but they could be in quite different segments of that market, depending for example on the type of food they serve, the prices they charge, the decor of the premises and quality of the service they offer. One could be a *cordon bleu* restaurant aimed at a high-spending clientèle, the other a 'greasy spoon' with its own type of clients. These are two similar business in quite different segments of the same marketplace.

COMPILING YOUR MARKET RESEARCH

How to compile your market research could almost be a book in itself – in fact there are already a number of books available on the subject. Your local book shop and library will have a wide selection for you to choose from. Market segmentation is just one area of your market research. Although important, it is even more important to look at your potential market as a whole.

Market research in its simplest form is the name given to the method of collating, storing, organising and assessing information about clients, competitors and any other ways they are influenced in the buying of products. Whether you are starting a new business or launching a new product or service, your research should be compiled before you embark fully on the project. In the long-term time spent on how to investigate your potential market will be time well spent, especially if you discover a major flaw in your idea or even worse find out that there is not even a market. At least then you could have only lost the time and energy it has taken to compile your data and not thousands of pounds in stock you cannot sell or a product that will be too expensive to manufacture.

Deciding your marketing objectives

The best way to begin your market research is to consider what information you want to discover from your research. Here are some questions for you to consider:

- What do your clients need from you?
- Who is your intended market and what information do you want to find out about them?
- Who and where are the competition and how do they compare to you?
- Are there any areas of the market you are able to exploit?
- Have you test marketed your product with your potential clients?

With these objectives in mind your market research will be clearly defined and will enable you to gain a better insight to the market you are in. Only when you are able to answer the above questions yourself will you be able to begin designing your questionnaire.

Types of market research

In the main there are two different types of market research for you to consider when you are about to start compiling your data. These are:

- field research;
- desk research.

Field research

This is obtained by collecting raw data from the general public as a whole and can take many different forms with one fundamental similarity, a questionnaire. The questionnaire will be developed from the information laid down in the marketing objectives and will be written with these in mind. Obviously, the information you want to discover from your market research will influence the questions asked and how they are worded.

1. The most common type of field research is that of personal interviews. These are usually conducted in the middle of the high street by an eager interviewer working on a commission to obtain as many completed questionnaires as they can.
2. Other methods of getting field research include interview by telephone, by post and by asking a company or group of individuals to use and test your product and then report back by completing a questionnaire.

Desk research

This involves analysing already-published data for you to adapt to suit the needs of your own marketing objectives. This was usually conducted at local reference libraries but the phenomenal growth and ease of the internet has almost rendered this method obsolete. The internet can be used to fully research an entire industry or a specific sector, product or service within an industry. The primary advantage of internet research is that results, information and statistics can be published and updated more frequently than through traditional publication methods. However, unless you have conducted the research yourself, then the golden rule with all research is always to question the integrity of the results by examining how the research was conducted. For example, was it independently produced or commissioned and could this have influenced the findings, how many people were questioned, how many products or services were tested and under what circumstances?

The sheer volume of data freely available on the internet means that you should be able to find, access and utilise what you are looking for, but for more specific results you may have to pay to access certain information. Depending on the provider and the depth of research, the price of this varies from a few pounds to hundreds of pounds. Only you can decide what level of research you need and how much you are prepared to pay.

Useful internet research sources

- Alacrawiki – www.alacrawiki.com
  A comprehensive guide to business information companies, publishers and databases.

- Kellys – www.kellysearch.co.uk
  A business-to-business product search engine to find UK industrial goods and service suppliers.

- Kompass – www.kompass.co.uk
  Offers a variety of locally-collected business information that can be used for a variety of purposes including research, sales, marketing and procurement.

- Market Research Portal – www.marketresearchworld.net
  An excellent market research resource providing free articles, findings, industry news and a useful glossary of marketing terms.

- Research Recap – www.researchrecap.com
  Collates a variety of free industry, economic, academic, market, investment and credit research reports and also provides links to relevant paid research.

- Trade Association Forum (TAF) – www.taforum.org
  Includes a searchable directory of UK trade associations. Some associations have useful statistics and free industry overviews.

Another useful research tool is Companies House which, for a small fee, can provide financial and other information about a variety of registered companies from its most recently filed accounts. Companies House can be contacted at www.companieshouse.gov.uk or by telephoning 0870 33 33 636.

DESIGNING YOUR QUESTIONNAIRE

There is not any particular right or wrong way to design a questionnaire. The layout and wording will be influenced by what information you want to discover. There are however some guidelines which you might find useful.

Guidelines

- Never ask any more questions than is absolutely necessary.
- Keep your questions short, simple and to the point.
- Your questions should be answerable with a simple yes, no, or do not know. If not, then offer a maximum of four alternatives.
- Not everyone interviewed will be a suitable respondent, so build in a question at the beginning of the questionnaire which will eliminate them from your research.
- Word your questions to get an exact answer, not just a vague one.
- Make the last question one that will show that a broad selection of respondents have been interviewed. Their occupation or salary are two good examples.

ANALYSING YOUR COMPETITION

The competition should always be treated with extreme caution. On one hand they are your enemy; they are the opposition who would like to see nothing better than you out of business. However, on the other hand they can be your best friend and you can learn just as much from them about how to successfully run your business as you can from any other source. As the old adage says, 'keep your friends close but keep your enemies even closer'.

The same rule should apply when you are in business. Who do your competitors buy from? How much do they buy? Who do they sell to? How much do they sell? The answers to these questions only barely begin to scratch the surface when you are analysing the competition but with these, and many other questions about your competitors and how they run their businesses, answered you will be well on the way to establishing your intended market and your clients.

Your competitors will come in many different shapes and sizes and their true identity will not always be apparent. In the main your competitors can be split into two categories:

- direct competitors;
- indirect competitors.

Direct competitors

These are defined as businesses which produce a similar product or offer a similar service to yours, and sell to a similar market to yours.

Indirect competitors

These are businesses which may either sell a different type of product or offer a different type of service to your business but in turn sell to a similar market. Alternatively, your indirect competitors may well sell similar products and offer a similar service but sell to a totally different market.

ANALYSING YOUR PRODUCT LIFE

No matter how big, small, old or new your product is, it will always abide by the laws of its product life. This in simple terms means charting the life of your product from the original concept and its introduction onto the market, through to market saturation, and eventual decline. Exactly where your products are positioned on the chart will depend on a number of factors including:

- How new or unique it is.
- Will clients continue to use your product after they have used it once?
- How will the competition react to your product and what steps will they take to maintain their own sales?
- Can your product be modified or further developed to prolong its life?

Product life cycle graph

Figure 1 illustrates an average sales pattern for two totally new products (A and B), from the early stages of their development through to their saturation of the market and then the decline as new products (A1) are introduced or the demand starts to decline due to a change in client-buying trends. As you can see, there are five main phases which attribute to the life of a product:

1. research and development;
2. introduction and launch;
3. growth and exploitation;
4. maturity and saturation;
5. decline and death.

SETTING YOUR SELLING PRICE

Many new businesses fail because they underprice themselves, nervous that the market will not pay their asking price. A lack of confidence in themselves and their new venture are the reasons for this but the golden rule is to always charge as much as the market is prepared to pay. It is common practice for new business to pitch their price just below the competition in an attempt to win over new clients who would have gone elsewhere.

Your selling price must be set with your competitors in mind so that even though you remain competitive within your market you are still able to make a profit. Your new product may be 10 times better than that of the competition but if you have got to charge ten times the price of your competitors in order to

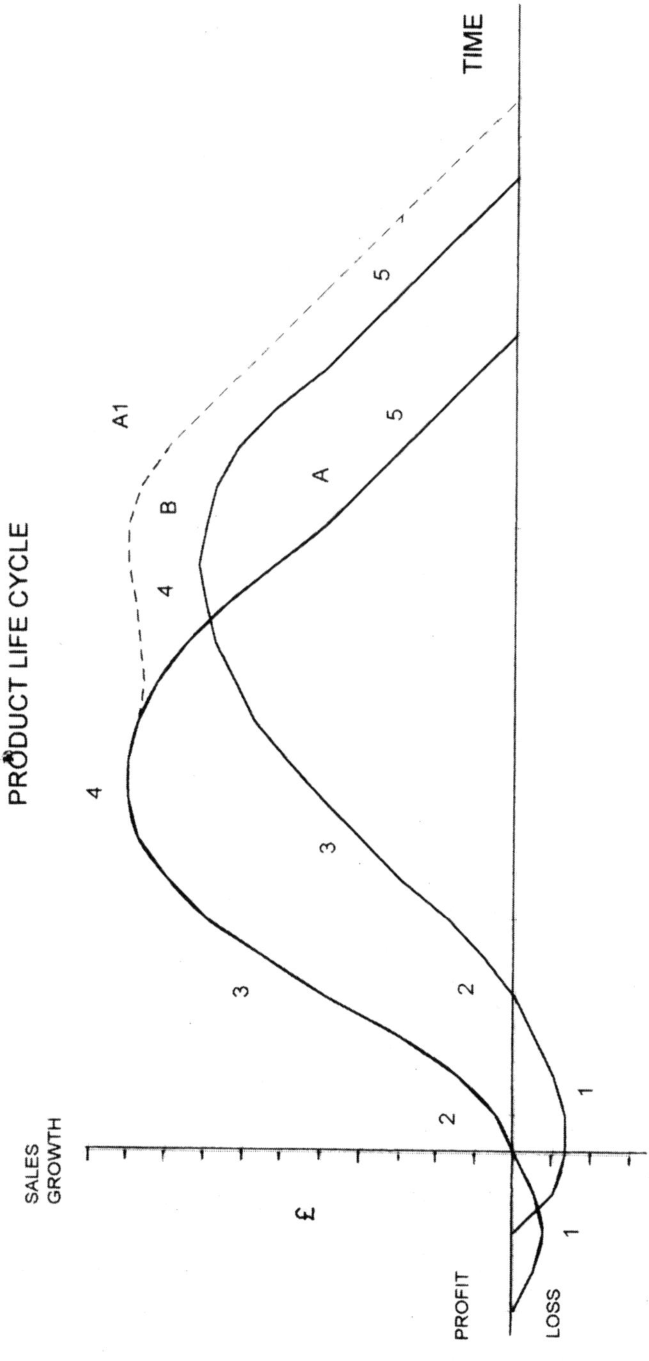

Fig. 1. A product life cycle graph.

make it profitable, then you must be sure that your clients will still be prepared to pay your selling price.

Pricing factors

When you set your selling price take into account every conceivable variable. It is not just a case of thinking of a number and then doubling or trebling it; there are many other factors to consider:

- Establishing the exact cost of producing your product by taking into account all of your overheads and the cost of your raw materials.
- What price the competition is asking for a similar product.
- Whether the demand for your product will affect your selling price; a cheaper price may increase the demand but this is not always the case.
- The image you are trying to convey. If you have a plush office in a new office block your selling price will be affected by your class of client whereas if you are based in a back street location your class of clientèle will probably be vastly different as will your selling price.
- Present market conditions. If you have developed a new safety product for children, and the media are currently featuring child safety, your selling price can be influenced by the fact there is already a great deal of client awareness about your product.
- Methods of distribution are important. Will you be sending your products nationwide or will your clients be calling to collect? The nature of your business will obviously affect this.
- Whether you are able to produce your products completely by yourself or if you will be contracting the work to an outside source.
- Assess your profit margin in relation to your costs. The retail sector traditionally works on a 100 per cent mark up by doubling the cost price of their stock but car dealers may only realise a 10 per cent profit margin on the sale of a new car.

Profitable pricing

Your selling price must be set so that you are able to make a profit and still remain competitive. Making a profit is the main reason for being in business. Unless you are actually making a profit then there is little point in operating your business in the first place. There is no set profit margin to use. Anything under 40 per cent of sales is going to mean you will have to make a lot of sales in order to keep your head above the water. If you are able to achieve and maintain anything above this amount then you will be doing very well. Your accountant and bank manager may have some knowledge of what margins would be typical in your business.

If you have discovered that at your current level of sales you were making a loss, it is important to understand how your profits will be affected by any changes you make to rectify this. Although the most obvious course of action would be to cut your selling price in an attempt to increase sales, this can actually make matters worse.

Pricing tables

Figure 2 shows two pricing tables. These can be used to work out by what percentage your level of sales can be reduced in the event of a price increase, or increased by in the event of a price decrease in order to maintain the same level of profitability. The tables have been reproduced by kind permission of TACK International, TACK House, Latimer Park, Chesham, Buckinghamshire HP5 1TR. Tel: 01494 766633. Fax: 01494 766622. Email: info@tack.co.uk or visit the TACK website at www.tack.co.uk

CHECKLIST

- Are you aware of exactly where your target market is?
- What area of your market will you concentrate on promoting and establishing your business in?
- Have you fully researched your intended potential market to ensure that your business can survive?

WHEN CONSIDERING INCREASING PRICES:

Present profit margin %

% PRICE RISE	10	15	20	25	30	35	40	50	60	70	80	90
2.0	17	12	9	7	6	5	5	4	3	3	2	2
3.0	23	17	13	11	9	8	7	6	5	4	4	3
4.0	29	21	17	14	12	10	9	7	6	5	5	4
5.0	33	25	20	17	14	12	11	9	8	7	6	5
7.5	43	33	26	23	20	18	16	13	11	10	9	8
10.0	50	49	33	29	25	22	20	17	14	12	11	10
15.0	60	50	43	37	33	30	27	22	20	18	16	14
20.0	67	57	50	44	40	37	33	29	25	22	20	18

% by which volume can go down without loss in sales revenue

WHEN CONSIDERING REDUCING PRICES (OR GIVING DISCOUNTS):

Present profit margin %

% PRICE REDUCTION	10	15	20	25	30	35	40	50	60	70	80	90
2.0	25	15	11	9	7	6	5	4	3	3	3	2
3.0	43	25	18	14	11	9	8	6	5	4	4	3
4.0	67	36	25	19	15	13	11	9	7	6	5	5
5.0	100	50	33	25	20	17	14	11	9	8	7	6
7.5	300	100	60	43	33	27	23	18	15	12	10	9
10.0	–	200	100	67	50	40	33	25	20	17	14	12
15.0	–	–	300	150	100	75	60	43	33	27	23	20
20.0	–	–	–	400	300	133	100	66	50	40	33	29

% by which volume must increase to maintain sales revenue

IMPORTANT NOTES:

This table takes no account of changes in Fixed Costs and Fixed Asset or Working Capital Investment arising from volume increases and therefore shows an absolute minimum.

This table may not be appropriate when dealing with 'fashion' goods or services which deteriorate or expire with time (newspapers, fruit and vegetables or an airline seat).

Fig. 2. Pricing tables.

- Are you aware of who your competitors will be and where they are positioned?
- Is the selling price you have set competitive and are you sure that your clients will pay it?

CASE STUDIES

Joshua and Jake prepare their business plan

The bank has provided Joshua and Jake with a pre-printed business plan form to complete before their forthcoming meeting. At first, compiling this lengthy document seems to be a daunting task. However, as they begin to read through it they soon realise most of the information can be extracted from a combination of the information pack supplied by the franchise company following their initial interest, and from the previous trading accounts of the present proprietor. Nevertheless, it takes many late nights and a lot of hard work before the document is complete. A letter of introduction is sent to the bank. After a reply by return of post, a date is set for the meeting.

Jasmine tests the local market

All Jasmine's market research shows that there is an untapped market niche for personalised calendars and diaries. However, before taking the plunge she decides to gauge the anticipated level of response by sending a mailshot to all large local companies with 20 or more employees.

She manages to obtain her mailing list from a local business directory. The mailshot announces the forthcoming launch of Calendar Creations and invites pre-launch orders at a discounted rate. Order forms are included with the mailing and then put on staff notice boards and in canteens. With the Christmas rush fast approaching the response is so tremendous that Jasmine wishes her business was already up and running.

Luke examines the grant options

Having carefully calculated how much additional finance would be required, Luke's next task is to decide how to obtain it. He decides his best option would be to look first at which government grants he may be eligible for, and then to raise the balance through private investment as opposed to a loan from the bank. During his investigations, Luke discovers that in his present town he would not qualify for any assistance. However, if he were to relocate his business to the next town then he could apply for a £200,000 relocation grant. In addition to this he could also borrow £100,000 at a heavily subsidised rate providing his grant application was approved.

Acton points

1. Describe which methods of research you will use to identify your potential market.
2. Assess the size of your potential market and the existing competitors. Will your business be able to survive and prosper?
3. Choose your selling price. How have you arrived at this figure?

4

Compiling Your Marketing Plan

Now that you have established exactly where and how big your potential market is, the next task is to put all your findings together in the form of objectives; these in turn will become your marketing plan. This marketing plan will form the basis of how you intend to promote your business and ensure that you are successful in generating sales revenue.

The nature of your business and the market you are in will influence what these objectives are. For example, a window cleaner may consider door-to-door canvassing and a small local advertising campaign to be a sufficient marketing plan. A larger electronics company will want to analyse current buying trends, establish the activity of their competitors and be constantly developing new products to stay ahead of the market as part of their marketing plan. If you are setting up an online business or using the internet to market your business then you will also need to sign up with an internet service provider (ISP) to test your website.

Making a SWOT analysis

Before you can begin to compile your marketing plan you need to make a critical self-assessment of where your business is and where you consider it to be going. This assessment is often known as the **SWOT analysis**. It must be brutally honest because if it is not, then the only person you will be fooling is yourself. The SWOT analysis relates to the following:

- Strengths;
- Weaknesses;

- Opportunities;
- Threats.

Strengths

The strengths of your business include everything that you are competent at, and everything associated with the running of your business from manufacturing and selling through to accountancy and purchasing. How many strengths you can describe as being competent in, will depend on whether you are a one-man band or if you have a number of employees able to strengthen your business.

Weaknesses

This is the most difficult section of the analysis to assess critically – but it is important to try. There will always be areas in which you lack the necessary expertise or experience whatever the size of your organisation. You may even need to approach an outside source and hire the necessary resources to get the job done.

Opportunities

It is very unlikely that you will ever be able to dominate your market. Even businesses seen as brand leaders are vulnerable to a competitor who discovers a gap in the market place.

Threats

Your competitors will present you with your biggest threat but they are far from representing the only one. For example, new legislation could be threatening, as could a change in client buying trends. Be aware of anything which may affect the success of your business. Let your reader know that you have identified these threats and how you intend to deal with them.

BALANCING YOUR MARKETING MIX

Marketing is a kind of chemistry. Putting together the right mix of marketing methods can make or break a business depending on whether you get the mix right or wrong. Having the right product, at the right price, in the right place, promoted by the best methods – is the basis for your marketing mix. Only by continuously changing and adapting your marketing mix to meet market trends will you be able to survive and progress.

Marketing can be divided into four sections, each linked integrally with one another. They will influence how you develop your marketing plan. These sections are often referred to as the four Ps of marketing and are as follows:

- product;
- price;
- place;
- promotion.

Product

This means what the product offers to the client in terms of features and benefits, quality, styling, guarantees and after-sales service.

Price

Value for money will be more important to the client than price alone but your selling price will depend on the client base, whether in the retail or trade sectors, and will depend on any special offers and your terms of sale, *eg* credit given and deposits.

Place

Where you and your distributors are located in relation to your clients, and what effect this has on your methods of distribution.

Promotion

The size of your business and your available advertising budget will affect how and where your business is best advertised. The cost of trade shows, web hosting, public relations, methods of selling and sales promotions are all covered under this section.

Getting the balance of the marketing mix can be likened to a set of scales: whatever adjustments you make on one section you will need to make a similar adjustment to another, or the scales of your marketing mix will overbalance and you could discover that your marketing plan has failed. For example, if you were to make a change to your selling price to increase the demand for your product, then you must also ensure that you adjust the product and place of your marketing mix so that you have sufficient supplies of your product in the right place to meet the expected demand.

DEFINING YOUR MARKETING OBJECTIVES

Now that you have defined your marketing mix, your next task is to clearly define your marketing objectives. These objectives and how you will achieve them through your marketing plan are closely linked with the overall business objectives that you have previously set. The recipient of your business plan must be able to understand what you want your marketing to achieve and how you intend to meet these objectives.

When you define your marketing objectives you can apply the same methods as you used to set your business objectives: examine the short-, medium- and long-term effects that your marketing will have on your business. This will show the reader of your plan that you have a clear vision of where your business is going and how you will take it there.

Short term

This generally means the immediate future and up to the end of your first year.

Medium term

The next two years are referred to as the medium term.

Long term

The long term is obviously more difficult to predict with any accuracy but your overall business strategy and objectives will affect what marketing methods you intend to be using in three to five years' time.

For each period of time list your objectives in the order in which you hope to achieve them, then follow your list of objectives with a strategy showing how these objectives will be achieved.

Example: the board game makers

The inventors and producers of a new board game might define their short-term marketing objectives as:

Objectives

1. Find a major wholesaler to take 50 per cent of production.
2. Expand a current local client base by creating an online presence.
3. Begin to develop a second board game for a similar target market.

Strategy

1. Develop a website and use public relations to launch the game by sending press releases to trade journals, magazines and newspapers.
2. Attend the London International Toy Fair in October to attract nationwide toy buyers.
3. Compile market research into the present games market to discover how to develop another winning game.

PROMOTING AND ADVERTISING YOUR BUSINESS

The steps you intend to take to promote your business will be just as important to the reader of your business plan as the product or service you will actually be selling. Now that the reader has grasped the concept of your business and what market you are in, he or she will now want to see exactly how you intend to make it all work.

The marketing methods that work for you will not necessarily be the same as those that work for your competitors. There is little point in advertising a certain way just because Joe Bloggs down the road does. The promotional methods that work for him and those that work for you will be the result of two different methods of marketing.

The promotional mix

The various ways to promote your business are known as the promotional mix and include:

- press advertising;
- direct mailing;
- public relations;
- exhibitions;
- the internet.

You will probably use one or a combination of all of these at some point.

Press advertising

Getting your message across and persuading the client to buy from you instead of the competition is the fundamental concept of advertising. To the small sole trader it can just mean having the van sign written and a few business cards printed. To the larger organisation it is likely to mean the start of a carefully thought-out and implemented strategy to increase sales.

The larger companies will be able to employ the services of an advertising agency. Before you rule this out as being too expensive it is well worth considering what they have to offer before you make any decision. Newly established agencies will probably be anxious for work (but do not mistake enthusiasm for experience).

If you decide to co-ordinate the advertising yourself, as many businesses do, then you will need to formulate a plan of where, when and how you will advertise. Start by asking yourself why you are advertising. What do you hope to achieve? Maybe you are just launching your business and want to advertise your presence or perhaps you are offering some kind of special promotion. The answer will form your advertising objectives.

Direct mailing

Direct mailing – or the 'mailshot' as it is more commonly known – can be a very effective method of advertising providing that your mailing is carefully **targeted** to achieve the maximum response. With the average response rate at a mere two per cent it is vital that your mailings only go to people who will be really interested in what you are offering.

Compiling a list of prospects

You can compile a list of potential prospects in a number of different ways including:

- Using published data in the form of trade journals, directories and yearbooks.
- Contacting mailing list brokers. These companies can supply address lists for any type of mailing from business opportunity seekers to gardening enthusiasts.
- Previous clients or inquiries: this type of list is likely to yield a better response rate than the other methods as half the work has already been done. Their interest has already been generated.

The mailshot format

Although the physical content of a mailshot will alter between businesses there is a standard format of what you should include:

- your sales letter;
- your sales literature;
- an easy method of ordering;
- a reply envelope or card.

Mailing lists

The Address Management Guide is an excellent source of useful mailing information and advice. It is produced by Royal Mail and covers everyday postal services through to specialist contract services for businesses. The guide can be ordered online from www.royalmail.com or by telephoning 08456 039038. Before embarking upon your direct mail campaign it may be worth contacting the Mailing Preference Service (MPS) who are a non-profit making body, established to foster good relations between direct mail users and the general public. The Mail Preference Service can be contacted at FREEPOST 29 LON20771, London W1E 0ZT. Tel: 0845 703 4599 (General Enquiries). Fax: 020

7323 4226. For further information email: mps@dma.org.uk Website: www.mpsonline.org.uk

Public relations

To appoint the services of a professional public relations consultancy used to be out of reach for most small businesses. However, there is now a variety of companies who specialise in providing a cost-effective solution in the form of fixed rate services which will enable you to plan your expenses more accurately.

Alternatively, with a little forethought and planning any company with commonsense can easily compile and implement their own public relations strategy. Public relations is a way for businesses to get their name in front of the public without actually paying to advertise. This can be done in a number of cost effective ways by:

- becoming a public speaker;
- sending letters to the editor of your trade journal or specialist magazine;
- getting a listing in yearbooks, trade directories and business publications;
- donating your time, products or money to a worthwhile charity;
- getting a regular slot on local television or radio;
- using announcement columns to tell the public what is new;
- compiling a press release to gain free publicity.

Of these various methods of public relations the most effective and frequently used is the press release.

Compiling a press release

A press release can be sent to any number of publications, including specialist business, trade and professional journals as well as local, regional and national newspapers and magazines. When you compile a press release, here are a few guidelines to help you increase your chances of publication.

1. Ensure your press release is double spaced typed for easy reading and no more than two pages long.
2. Your press release must be newsworthy and appeal to the editor. Avoid trying to sell your product or service or your release will end up in the bin.
3. Observe the who, what, where, when, why and how principle of journalism. If your press release covers all these points it will improve your chance of publication.
4. Your headline will either make or break the chance of getting published so think long and hard before committing yourself to your headline. Editors are looking for original, appealing or humorous headlines.
5. Always include a contact name, address and telephone number with your release or your release will not even be considered.
6. Make sure you address your press release to the editor of the relevant publication unless it states otherwise.

Exhibitions

Although these can be a costly expense if you intend to actually exhibit at one, exhibitions can prove to be an excellent source of information for both potential clients and competitors alike. Your competitors will be able to visit your stand and see exactly what you have to offer. As this is a two-way street, you will be able to do the same, and analyse and assess the competition all under one roof.

For new and existing businesses, exhibitions can be a great way to launch their company or new products straight into the mainstream of sales with both buyers and distributors being able to view what you are selling. Never underestimate the power of an exhibition as a tremendous wealth of information and inspiration.

There are many companies who specialise in designing and preparing everything necessary for the perfect exhibition stand. In addition to this there are a number of companies who are able to supply visual aids and exhibition equipment including:

Nobo Visual Aids Ltd, Alder Close, Compton Industrial Estate, Eastbourne, Sussex BN23 6QB. Tel: 01323 641521.

Pinewood Associates, Hardy Street, Manchester M30 7NN. Tel: 0161 7076000. Fax: 0161 7076766. Email: sales@pinewoodassociates.com Website: www.pinewoodassociates.com

The internet

Using the internet to promote and advertise your business is an excellent way to generate sales and increase your awareness. A website can be used to sell online, reach international markets, promote your business to a wider customer base and generate additional sales from current customers. It can also be used to save time and money by answering common queries, eliminating the need to produce printed brochures, communicate by email and even advertise for new staff.

However, depending on the size and nature of your business, setting up a website can be a daunting task. This is particularly true if you are setting up an online store with many different and changing product lines. The first stage of web design is to think about the content of your site, which can be done by asking your existing customers about what they would like to see on your site, or by comparing those of your competitors. At the very least you should have:

- an information 'Home Page' clearly illustrating what you do;
- an 'About Us' page with a little company background;
- a detailed 'Contact' page with your address, phone, fax and email details.

You could also consider:

- incorporating a 'Site Map' to direct visitors;
- adding a 'Search' facility to help visitors find what they are looking for;
- including a series of frequently asked questions (FAQs) to reduce repetitive customer enquiries.

If you are going to trade online then you will also need to add the following:

- a privacy policy describing how personal information is handled;
- details of your quality guarantee together with a clear exchange, returns and refund policy;
- postage, packing and delivery costs;
- accurate price and details of product availability.

Constructing your website

If you just want a basic website to promote your company and your contact details then this can be done with a simple web design program. A quick internet search will reveal that there are many to choose from. Some can be downloaded for free and will offer basic tools and templates. Others will need to be purchased, but they will offer more advanced features. If your website is more complex then you may need to use a website designer. This can be quite expensive but a professionally designed site should help you attract sufficient business to offset the initial design costs. Once again, an internet search will reveal many different web design companies to choose from.

Registering your web (domain) name

To prevent other companies from using your intended domain name, it is important to register it as soon as you can. There are many different registration companies to choose from and annual prices vary between £2 and £4 for each domain extension. Popular business extensions include .co.uk, .org.uk, .com, .net, .info and .biz and it is advisable to register as many of these as you can because there is nothing to stop somebody else legally registering a non-registered extension. Most companies also offer a variety of web hosting and web promotion options so it is worth shopping around for a package deal. Popular companies include:

www.123-reg.co.uk	123-reg
www.123domainnames.co.uk	123 Domain Names UK
www.cheapdomain.co.uk	Cheap Domain Names

www.names.co.uk	Names Co
www.uk2.net	UK2

Promoting your website

This is a very important part of the process because in order to attract internet traffic, major search engines such as Ask.com, Google and Yahoo need to know of your existence. This is achieved by uploading a series of keywords with your website that search engines will use to guide users to your site. Most web designers will include a degree of marketing and promotional activity within their fee and nearly all web design programs have similar tools built into them. Another way to increase your profile is to create a hotlink from your website to another similarly themed but non-competitive company or organisation and ask them to do the same. For example, if you offer a dog walking service you could create hotlinks to dog trainers, groomers, vets and kennels and ask them to do the same.

MONITORING THE RESPONSE

Whichever marketing methods you decide will work for your business, it is only by constantly reviewing, amending and adapting your strategies that your business will succeed. A method of marketing that you use today could very well be out of date within a short period of time. Therefore, it is essential to keep monitoring which methods are most cost effective.

Before you can begin to monitor your responses you must obviously have all the information to hand. This can be done by finding out where your clients heard about you by simply asking them as they make an enquiry or sale. As long as you know the cost of using a particular method of advertising or marketing, and know how many clients and sales have been generated from it, then you can analyse which methods are the most cost effective.

CHECKLIST

- What do you want your marketing to achieve and how will go you about it?

- Have you described the marketing methods you will use to advertise and promote your business?
- Can you state the strengths and weaknesses of your competitors and how your business can satisfy the needs of your clients?
- Can you state the size of your potential market and what share you hope to achieve after your initial trading period?
- Who will use your product or service? How often will they purchase and how much will they be prepared to pay?
- Have you compiled your marketing strategy with a plan of how you will attain your objectives?
- Have you worked out a way of monitoring your marketing methods to see which methods are the most effective?

CASE STUDIES

Joshua and Jake face a setback

Joshua and Jake go to their meeting with the bank manager full of hope and confidence, safe in the knowledge that they have completed their business plan to the bank's specifications. By now both are anxious to get the loan approved and begin their business relationship. The business is profitable and looks to remain that way; the asking price is fair and they have already committed their own savings to the proposal. Nothing can go wrong – or so they think.

The bank manager looks favourably on their proposal and even agrees that should he ever lose his job, he might even consider a similar opportunity himself. The projections look good, and provided the present level of sales revenue could be maintained, then the repayments should easily be met.

However, the bank is keen to learn how their repayments are to be met, should the level of sales fall below the estimates. As neither Joshua nor Jake has any equity in their homes or any other form of security, the bank has little option but to turn down their application for an unsecured loan. It was a risk the bank was not prepared to take no matter how good the proposal looked on paper.

Jasmine prepares her business plan

Despite all the positive response, Jasmine decides that she will still need a business plan to explain how her business will survive. She realises that the interest so far has been heavily influenced by the Christmas rush – but how will she survive during the rest of the year? Calendars are traditionally only purchased once a year, so she will need to discover a way to survive during the interim period.

Further research indicates that large organisations begin to purchase calendars in June ready for December. Jasmine's business plan shows that if she could achieve a minimum of 20 per cent of her total sales revenue for the second half of the year in the first half, then her business would prosper. This could be achieved by targeting clubs and societies with summer fixtures and timetables such as skittles, bowls and darts leagues. These organisations would place orders during the early part of the year, and this would boost revenue. With this information to hand and her business objectives clearly defined within her business plan, Jasmine decides to launch Calendar Creations.

Luke seeks additional finance

Having calculated how much grant assistance he would be eligible for, Luke still needs to raise an additional £100,000. With his business already achieving a £2 million turnover – set to increase by at least 25 per cent with the new contract – raising the additional finance should not prove too difficult. In exchange for the necessary £100,000, Luke offers the investor a 10 per cent share of his business and a yearly dividend.

Action points

1. Select the methods you want to use to promote your business.
2. Devise a press release launching your new business venture.
3. Look at the methods your competitors use to promote and advertise their businesses. What are the advantages and disadvantages to using these methods?

5

Your Operational Plan

Now that you have considered the various strategies to ensure the success of your venture, it is important for the reader of your plan to understand *how* you intend to meet these objectives. Your **operations** plan is another term for the 'nuts and bolts' of your business. It is the behind-the-scenes work that is needed to make your business successful.

CHOOSING YOUR CHANNELS OF DISTRIBUTION

In an ideal world all of your clients would come directly to you, eliminating all your distribution costs. Deciding which method of distribution to use would not even be an issue. However, whatever the size of your business, you can assume at some point you will have to address the issue of distribution. How you intend to distribute your product or service to your clients will depend on a number of factors, including your profit margin and selling price.

There are three methods of distribution for you to consider:

- indirect distribution;
- direct distribution;
- third party distribution.

Indirect distribution

If your product will be sold through the retail and wholesale sectors then this is considered to be indirect distribution as your clients will be purchasing your product from a business other than yours. Only products with a large profit margin and mass appeal tend to be sold in this way. With a large profit margin you will be able to attract good distributors with a generous discount whilst still keeping a percentage of the profits for yourself.

Direct distribution

Products which are sold straight from yourself to your clients are described as being distributed directly. This is usually achieved when you use the internet or telephone for selling and then back it up with a mail order method of distribution, or when the client comes to your premises.

Third party distribution

Appointing an agent to sell your products on your behalf is another method of distribution. This method is favoured by businesses such as double glazing and insurance companies, but their heavy handed, hard sell techniques have often brought door-to-door selling a bad name, and resulted in the introduction of new legislation to cut down on cowboy companies.

A softer approach has been made by direct selling companies such as Avon, Betterware and Kleeneze which have proved to be a very successful way of selling. Further information and advice about direct selling can be obtained from Direct Selling Association, 29 Floral Street, London WC2E 9DP. Tel: 020 7497 1234. Fax: 020 7497 3144. Email: info@dsa.org.uk Website: www.dsa.org.uk

FINDING THE RIGHT PREMISES

The location of your business will partly depend on what you are selling, and who to. For example, if you have a restaurant or a retail store then your clients will be coming to you. However, the manufacturing industry will generally discover its potential market and then go out and sell to it. In this case your channels of distribution will have an effect on where your business is located as will the possibility of obtaining a grant.

If your business is located in a rural or undeveloped area then you may be eligible to receive a grant from the European Commission, UK Government, local government, corporate sponsors or charitable trusts. For further information contact the rural development network at ruralnet|uk, National Rural Enterprise Centre, Stoneleigh Park, Kenilworth, Warwickshire CV8 2RR.

Tel: 0845 1300 411. Fax: 0845 1300 433. Email: enquiries@ruralnetuk.org Website: www.ruralnetuk.org

Alternatively contact Make Your Mark at 6 Mercer Street, Covent Garden, London WC2H 9QA. Tel: 020 7497 4030. Email: info@makeyourmark.org.uk Website: www.makeyourmark.org.uk

Make Your Mark is the national campaign to create an enterprise culture among young people in the UK by helping to provide inspiration and opportunity to turn their ideas into reality. However, their website contains a very useful list of links to a variety of grants and funding opportunities.

Positioning your business

Your market research data will show where the best position of your business is in relation to your intended market. In reality, this can be easier to discover than to put into practice. Retail stores generally prefer to be in the middle of a busy high street, whilst a manufacturing business might favour a purpose-built unit on an industrial site. A new business may find it difficult to meet the running costs of being in such a prime position.

Alternatively, consider setting up an online business. This type of business tends to have lower start-up and running costs than a traditional business.

Where you are positioned in relation to your competition will affect your success. Will you be attracting trade away from your competitors by competing close to them? Or will the fact that you are the only type of business in a particular area be one of your benefits? Only you will be able to discover the answers to these questions.

MEETING SAFETY AND QUALITY STANDARDS

If your business involves the manufacturing or assembly of products then you need to be aware that your products may have to meet one or more of the many standards of safety and quality set by the British Standards Institute. Tell the reader of your business plan about any standards your business has to comply with, and how you will obtain the relevant certification.

There are approximately 27,000 BSI British Standards covering everything from accounting to zoom lenses. Depending on their complexity, the cost of a BSI standard ranges from £5 to £1,150. The most popular standard in the world is *ISO 9001 Quality Management Systems – Requirements* which is used by more than 670,000 organisations in 154 countries. ISO 9001 certification does not guarantee the quality of products but relates to the internal paperwork procedures prescribed by the standard. Many organisations use ISO 9001 certification as an effective marketing tool to promote themselves as a well organised business with clearly defined procedure and protocols.

Further information and advice about registration and certification can be obtained from BSI British Standards, 389 Chiswick High Road, London W4 4AL. Tel: 020 8996 9001. Fax: 020 8996 7001. Email: cservices@bsigroup.com Website: www.bsi-global.com

Depending on the nature of your business and the intended market for your product or service, you may need to apply for a BSI Kitemark certification. These are used to guarantee that your products or services conform to the most rigorous of quality processes. Some certification schemes are mandatory and are subject to enforcement by law, whereas others are voluntary and are undertaken to demonstrate the quality of a product or service to gain a market advantage.

Further information about certification and marks can be obtained from BSI Product Services, Kitemark House, Maylands Avenue, Hemel Hempstead HP2 4SQ. Tel: 0845 0765600. Fax: 0845 0765601.

OBTAINING STOCK AND MATERIALS

Having sufficient stock to sell is obviously crucial to the success of your business and your business plan should set out the methods you will use to obtain your products. Your reader will not expect you to go into great detail, just to summarise how your stock will finally be made ready for sale.

If you will be buying your stock as fully assembled products then tell the reader your sources of supply and how they compare with other businesses supplying similar products. Explain how your stock will get to you, how long it will take and what conditions of sale will be made such as sale or return and whether you will be granted any credit. However, if your products will be bought in as partially assembled products then you will need to explain your manufacturing process, stating how this stock will become assembled into your finished products.

Learning from competitors

It is worth investigating how and where your competitors obtain their materials. They have probably been established for a number of years and are fully aware of which suppliers are better than others. Constantly monitor the quality of your materials because you will only ever be as good as the materials you use.

- Keep it simple – Remember to make your business plan easy to read by eliminating any complicated jargon and substituting it with easy to understand terms.

CONTROLLING YOUR LEVEL OF QUALITY

Unless you are planning to buy an already established business your first objective will be to convince your potential clients of the quality of your product. Quality is of paramount importance and should never be overlooked. It not only relates to your finished product or service but it encompasses the whole concept of your business.

Every point of contact your clients have with your business will be measured in terms of the quality of your business. Whether it is on the telephone, over the internet, with face-to-face contact or by postal correspondence, how you present yourself and your business will constantly be assessed in terms of the level of service your clients will demand and expect.

Remember, just as a chain is only as strong as its weakest link, so is a business. You may have a product or service that is second to none in terms of quality and value for money but if your website is poorly constructed or if clients contact you by telephone and are greeted by a miserable unhelpful voice, then you will not get the chance to show how good your business really is.

Maintaining quality

Once you have established a level of quality it is important to maintain it. Don't fall into the same trap as certain other companies by becoming complacent and allowing the standards you have set to become only adequate. We are living in a fast moving world; by tomorrow, today's level of quality could be out of date. Constantly monitor your quality, and your previous, current and potential clients will be able to help you achieve this objective. Constant communication with your clients is the key to maintaining the level of quality and service they have come to expect. How will you be able to put a problem right if you are not even aware that a problem exists in the first place? Your clients should be the first to let you know when there is a problem, unless of course you can foresee any decline in quality and already have a strategy to overcome it.

EMPLOYING YOUR KEY PERSONNEL

Your personnel are the most important element of your business plan. Without them you will cease to have a business to run.

- In this section of your business plan you should highlight the job descriptions of each key member of staff.

Once you become fully operational your staff are in any case required by law to be given a written job description and a contract of employment stating the terms and conditions of the position offered. In the event of any dispute both parties then have a written document to refer to.

After you have defined your key personnel you will be in a better position to assess whether your present level of staffing is adequate and if not then how you will overcome this. Your level of staffing should be sufficient to cover holidays, sickness and days off without affecting the smooth running of your business. You may decide to alter the job descriptions of your present staff to compensate for any shortfall or perhaps employ further members of staff. Alternatively, you may consider introducing a number of training programmes to let your present personnel develop the skills and experience needed for your business.

The reader of your business plan will want to know about your employment methods. Will you advertise nationally or locally for staff? What wage and salary will you be offering? What, if any, incentives can your personnel expect to receive such as pensions, profit and performance related bonuses, holidays or other personal benefits?

Your reader will also want to know about any provisions you have made for the payment of PAYE (Pay As You Earn), National Insurance and pension schemes. Becoming a new employer can be a daunting task but to ease the process, HM Revenue & Customs (HMRC) have produced an informative New Employer Starter Park which offers a step-by-step approach to all of the forms and procedures required to organise your payroll. The pack also includes an Employer CD-ROM which can help you to calculate tax and National Insurance deductions easily. To order a pack visit the HMRC website at www.hmrc.gov.uk or telephone the HMRC New Employer Helpline on 0845 6070143. Helpline staff will also be able to answer any general queries that you have regarding tax, National Insurance and VAT registration.

As an employer, you are not obliged to set up a pension scheme but depending on the size of your business you may be required to provide access to a third party scheme. For further advice contact the Pensions Advisory Service, 11 Belgrave Road, London SW1V 1RB. Tel: 0845 6012923. Fax: 020 7233 8016. Email: enquiries@pensionsadvisoryservice.org.uk Website: www.pensionsadvisory service.org.uk

ORGANISING YOUR BOOK-KEEPING

In your business plan you will need to cover the question of book-keeping. Tell your reader what methods you intend to use and who will be responsible for ensuring that the books are up to date. Chapter 10 takes a more in-depth look at what is involved with keeping accounts. In the meantime it is important to understand why your book-keeping is important and what effect inadequate accounts will have on your business.

When any new business is launched, a capital investment is made to get the business started. This investment will be used to acquire various items needed to get things going. In turn this will lead to a return on the capital investment by generating sales revenue to come into the business.

All movements of money coming into and going out of the business must be fully documented and recorded. This is achieved by keeping a set of organised books detailing all transactions. If you run a larger business then you may be able to employ a book-keeper to control the books for you. However, if you run a smaller business, the responsibility of maintaining accurate and up-to-date books will remain with you personally.

INSURING YOURSELF AND YOUR BUSINESS

Regardless of the size and nature of your business you will need to make sure that you and your business have sufficient insurance should anything go wrong. There are many different types of insurance. Some are mandatory (required by law) such as motor insurance and employer's liability insurance if you have any employees. Others will depend on the nature of your business, and are largely a matter of common sense – policies such as cover against fire, theft and accidental damage.

Your business plan need not go into great detail about your intended policies, such as who they are with or what they will cost. Your reader will only be interested to learn that you *are* planning to be adequately insured. A good business insurance broker who knows the job inside out will be worth their weight in gold in finding the best quotes for the specific cover you will need for your business.

Getting independent advice

The golden rule to remember when dealing with insurance is always to seek professional independent advice. Some insurance companies will sell you policies that you simply do not need. Make sure that your insurance broker is a member of the British Insurance Brokers' Association which is the UK's leading independent insurance body, representing both the insurance broker, intermediaries and the consumer. Further information can be obtained from British Insurance Brokers' Association (BIBA), 14 Bevis

Marks, London EC3A 7NT. Tel: 0901 8140015 (Consumer Helpline). Fax: 020 7626 9676. Email: enquiries@biba.org.uk Website: www.biba.org.uk

CHECKLIST

- Do you know the channels of distribution you will use to get your product or service to your clients?
- Have you selected the right business premises for your potential market?
- Will any alterations be needed to the premises before you can start trading and has any necessary permission been sought from the local authorities?
- Does your business need to be registered with any authorities and has this been done?
- Do you know who your main suppliers will be, and what their terms and conditions of sale are?
- What steps have to be taken to ensure that your level of quality will be maintained?
- Have you considered who your key members of staff will be and have they been appointed?
- Have you made plans to keep your accounts from day one and decided who will be responsible to ensure that they are kept up to date?
- Do you and your business have an adequate level of insurance cover to provide for every eventuality?

CASE STUDIES

Joshua and Jake discover the Small Firms Loan Guarantee scheme

Whilst using the internet to research alternative finance opportunities, Jake discovered information about the Small Firms Loan Guarantee (SFLG) scheme. Joshua and Jake feel that the business will be profitable and all projections indicate that this would continue but they still have to overcome the problem of loan security. To borrow any money from friends or family would still leave them with the same debts but from a different source.

At the local library Jake discovered a book about raising finance which mentioned the government's Small Firms Loan Guarantee Scheme. Under the scheme, 75 per cent of the loan would be guaranteed by the government for a business such as Joshua and Jake's in exchange for a small guarantee premium. This meant that should the business fail, then 75 per cent of the loan would be repaid by the government which would leave the bank with only 15 per cent of the loan unsecured.

Jasmine launches Calendar Creations

Calendar Creations is launched just in time for the Christmas rush. As the business begins to get established it becomes apparent that Jasmine's original projections were a little too conservative. Although it was quite an effort Jasmine has managed to fulfil all her obligations and get the calendars out on time.

After Christmas the rush did not really die down as more and more people began to hear about her and her business through word-of-mouth recommendations. Orders started coming in for summer league fixture cards, school diaries for the new academic year, and from a broad selection of clubs and societies. Jasmine's business was by far surpassing her original expectations – wonderful!

Luke prepares his business plan

Having found the avenue of additional capital investment, Luke's next job was to compile his business plan in such a way as to satisfy both the government grant board and his potential investor that he was offering a viable opportunity. He did this by generalising the facts and figures relating to the current business as a whole, and then highlighting the specific details which related to the grant board and to the private investor. This had the double benefit of not only illustrating to the government where the additional investment would be coming from but also showing the potential investor how the government would be assisting.

Action points

1. List the various methods of distribution of goods and services to customers. What are the advantages and disadvantages of the method that you will choose?

2. Describe the proposed location of your business. What, if any, effect will this have on the level of your expected sales revenue?

3. Examine the different types of business insurance policies.

6

Your Sales Forecast

So far your business plan has told the reader what you are selling, who you are selling it to and how you intend to generate these sales. Now it is time to put all of your assumptions together in the form of your sales forecast. This represents the most important set of figures to come out of your business plan to date. These figures will be used to compile your cashflow, profit and loss and balance sheet forecasts. In addition they will be used to calculate how much capital you will need to get started, how much profit you expect to make and ultimately the viability of your business venture.

PROJECTING YOUR SALES

When you compile your expected sales projections, make sure the figures you present really are achievable, believable and most of all realistic. If your business is in the fortunate position of already having advance orders then you may already have a good idea of what your sales will be. However, if you are launching a new venture then your assumptions will be based on the information you have gathered from your market research studies. It is inevitable that the enthusiasm you have for your venture will lead you to be a little optimistic with your projections but try to keep yourself focused on a believable and prudent forecast.

Making up a sales forecast

Whatever sales projections you make you must be able to support your assumptions with evidence clearly showing how these figures will be reached. There are various methods you can use to support your sales projections including:

- gathering sales information on similar businesses;
- communicating with the founders of similar indirect competitors;
- discovering how much revenue your target market generates and what market share you hope to achieve;
- analysing previous sales records, if the business is already established;
- listing any firm orders that you have already received.

COMPILING YOUR PROFIT AND LOSS FORECAST

Your profit and loss forecast will show your potential investors or backers just how viable your venture is in terms of its profitability. You will find it very difficult to get any kind of capital investment unless you can show that at some point your sales will exceed the costs incurred for obtaining that sales revenue, and that your business is trading at a profit. A typical profit and loss forecast will be budgeted on a monthly basis for the first 12 months, and then quarterly for the following two years assuming you feel confident enough to predict that far.

Most of the banks and financial institutions will be able to provide their own standard profit and loss forecast forms similar to the one shown in Figure 3, reproduced by kind permission of Barclays Bank plc. In order to compile a full 12-month forecast, simply carry forward the subtotals column to complete the remaining six months. The nature of your business will determine which of these headings will apply, so just leave blank any columns that are not applicable. It is worth remembering that the figures you enter into your profit and loss forecast will be exclusive of any VAT.

Budgeted sales

Your sales forecast will have shown how much sales revenue you expect your business to generate. You can now begin putting these figures into the 'budget' column of your profit and loss forecast.

Profit & Loss Forecast Year

*	Month		Month		Month
	Budget	Actual	Budget	Actual	Budget
Sales (a)					
Less: Direct Costs					
Cost of Materials					
Wages					
Gross Profit (b)					
Gross Profit Margin (b/a x 100%)					
Overheads					
Salaries					
Rent/Rates/Water					
Insurance					
Repairs/Renewals					
Heat/Light/Power					
Postages					
Printing/Stationery					
Transport					
Telephone					
Professional Fees					
Interest Charges					
Other					
Other					
Total Overheads (c)					
Trading Profit (b) - (c)					
Less: Depreciation					
Net Profit Before Tax					

*These headings may vary according to the needs of your business. You may therefore need to amend any that are not app

Fig. 3. A profit and loss forecast.

beginning________________

BARCLAYS

	Month		**Month**		**Month**		**Sub totals**	
Actual	Budget	Actual	Budget	Actual	Budget	Actual	Budget	Actual

licable.

PTO

1. If you are planning to set up a new business, remember to allow for a steady build up of sales during your initial trading period.
2. Your forecast should also allow for any seasonal influences which will affect the demand for your product or service.
3. For your profit and loss forecast your sales should include all the work you have completed or invoiced regardless of whether or not you have been paid. At present you are only concerned with the profitability of your venture, not its cashflow.

Budgeted direct costs

To calculate your direct (variable) costs simply add together the cost of the materials you have used, with the cost of the labour you have engaged to either make, buy or offer sufficient goods or services to meet your monthly sales figure.

Budgeted gross profit

You can calculate your gross profit by deducting the total of your direct costs from your sales figures.

Gross profit margin (%)

Dividing your gross profit by your total sales and then multiplying this figure by 100 will give you your percentage gross profit margin. For example:

$$\frac{\text{GP: } \pounds\ 43{,}000}{\text{Sales: } \pounds 100{,}000} \times 100 = 43\%$$

Total overheads

Your total overheads (fixed or semi-variable costs) incorporate every expense associated with the running of your business. Unlike your direct costs which vary according to output, your overheads are likely to remain fixed for the duration of your business but will increase with inflation and if your business expands.

Working through the list of overheads, estimate the annual cost of each one and then divide by 12 to give your average total monthly expense. Quarterly expenses such as telephone, gas and electricity should be included in this monthly figure. Remember, your cashflow forecast will detail exactly *when* they have to be paid. Your profit and loss forecast merely allows you to budget for them.

Trading profit

Subtracting your total monthly overheads from your monthly gross profit will provide you with your trading profit. If your gross profit is larger than your overheads then your business will be trading at a profit. However, the reader of your business plan will probably be surprised to see anything other than a forecast loss during your initial trading period while your sales have time to catch up with your expenses.

Depreciation

You can only 'depreciate' business assets which you own such as plant and equipment. You do not depreciate any assets which are rented, hired or leased.

The best way to calculate your monthly depreciation figure is to begin with the purchase cost of each asset and then divide this by the amount of years which you consider it will be able to be used within the business. For example a £1,000 computer system with an expected lifespan of five years will depreciate at a rate of £200 per annum. Dividing your yearly depreciation by 12 will give your monthly figure to include in your forecast.

Interest

You will also have to forecast the interest payable on any loans and bank overdraft that you may have.

Net profit before tax

To complete your profit and loss forecast simply deduct your monthly depreciation figure from your trading profit to give your net profit before tax.

Backing up your figures

It will not be enough to submit your profit and loss forecast on its own merit. Your reader will expect to see evidence of how you arrived at all your figures. A set of notes which explain the reasons behind your assumptions will help to convince your reader that you have carefully considered your forecast and not just entered a series of numbers at random. Any information you have included about price lists, guaranteed orders or supplier quotations should be included in your notes and then referenced within your appendices.

DRAFTING YOUR CASHFLOW FORECAST

As your cashflow and profit and loss forecasts are very similar in appearance and layout you should apply the same principles when you are completing both of them. To begin with, all of the figures that you include must be substantiated with supplementary notes explaining how you arrived at them and where appropriate, with material to back up your forecasts. Your cashflow forecast is a working example which shows the expected effects on your bank balance over a period of time, and your ability to pay your creditors as money moves into and out of your business account. It will also show when any additional finance may be required and when it could be repaid.

Most of the figures for your cashflow forecast will be the same as those you have already used for your profit and loss forecast. It is just a case of transferring these figures into your cashflow forecast.

Using the cashflow forecast illustrated in Figure 4 (again reproduced with kind permission of Barclays Bank plc) you can see that many of the headings mirror those of the profit and loss forecast with just a few differences. In order to compile a full 12-month forecast, simply carry forward the subtotals column to complete the remaining six months. Working down through the forecast you will start with your receipts.

Receipts

Your sales will change over time as your products move through their life cycle where a peak is reached and then sales either subside or decline. Whenever a peak in sales occurs, sales thereafter will either subside (level out) as repeat orders are received or products are supplied in direct line with demand or they will decline as competitors begin to supply similar products or demand for the product has fallen – toys are a good example of this. Allow for these peaks and dips within your figures by regular monitoring of your business. It is important to note that, if applicable, your sales figure should include the VAT that you have charged. VAT can be a big item in a cashflow forecast.

Your cash sales estimate will be similar to the figure you used for profit and loss forecast providing that most of your clients will pay with cash. Of the clients to whom you extend credit and invoice, a 10 per cent non payment factor would be a realistic average to work to. Whenever your debtors (people who owe you money) make a payment you should record this under the 'cash from debtors' column.

There may be times in the life of your business that you will make additional payments into your account. These could be in the form of savings, loans, grants or even receipts from the sales of any assets. Whenever you make such a payment it should be included in the 'capital introduced' column. Your 'total receipts' is the total of all of these figures.

Payments

Your payments represent *all* of the expenses that will be going out of the business. In an ideal world all of your debtors would pay up promptly and all of your creditors (people to whom you owe money) would offer you an extended line of credit. In turn this would lead to a very healthy bank account and put you in an excellent cashflow position.

However, back in the real world this just does not happen so it is important for the survival of your business to reach a happy medium. This can be done by delaying your outgoing payments for as long as you reasonably can without triggering any bankruptcy orders against you, whilst at the same time maintaining tight credit control of your debtors.

Salaries and wages

This figure must include all National Insurance and Pay As You Earn (PAYE) payments you may have to pay on behalf of your staff. If your business trades as a sole trader or partnership then any money you pay yourself will be classed as **drawings** as opposed to a salary or wage. It should still be included in this figure and mentioned in your accompanying notes.

Cashflow Forecast Year

* Receipts	Month Budget	Month Actual	Month Budget	Month Actual	Month Budget
Cash Sales					
Cash from Debtors					
Capital Introduced					
Total Receipts (a)					
Payments					
Payments to Creditors					
Salaries/Wages					
Rent/Rates/Water					
Insurance					
Repairs/Renewals					
Heat/Light/Power					
Postages					
Printing/Stationery					
Transport					
Telephone					
Professional Fees					
Capital Payments					
Interest Charges					
Other					
VAT payable (refund)					
Total Payments (b)					
Net Cashflow (a-b)					
Opening Bank Balance					
Closing Bank Balance					

*These headings may vary according to the needs of your business. You may therefore need to amend any that are not app

Fig. 4. A cashflow forecast.

beginning ____________________

BARCLAYS

	Month		Month		Month		Sub totals	
Actual	Budget	Actual	Budget	Actual	Budget	Actual	Budget	Actual

licable.

PTO

Most of the remaining headings under the payments section will be the same as they were in the profit and loss account. However, it may be possible to take advantage of a monthly direct debit system that many utility and insurance companies are now in favour of. This will mean you will not be faced with any unexpected bills once a quarter: you will be able to forecast your cashflow with more accuracy as you will know in advance what most of your payments will be.

Interest charges

This will only apply if your business is either being operated with an overdraft facility or you have taken out any loans. The bank will charge you on a quarterly or monthly basis straight from your business account.

VAT payable

You will only have to be registered for VAT by law if your annual sales exceed £64,000. VAT is split into two sections; there is the VAT that you charge to your clients (**outputs**), and the VAT that you pay to your suppliers (**inputs**). The difference between these two amounts represents the money you owe to HM Revenue & Customs if your outputs are greater than your inputs (and vice versa). This total will either be paid or received on a monthly or quarterly basis and should be included in your forecast.

Total payments

The next task is to add together all of these figures to give the total of your monthly payments.

Net cashflow

To calculate your net flow of cash simply subtract your total monthly payments from your total monthly receipts. Any minus figure should be identified by putting brackets around the amount, for example (£432).

Bank balance

Your net cashflow total must either be added or subtracted (depending on whether the amount is a plus or minus) from your opening bank balance, to give you your closing bank balance.

Finishing off

Just as you provided supplementary notes for your profit and loss forecast, the same must be done for your cashflow forecast. The reader of your business plan will not be too pleased to receive a comprehensive forecast without any explanation of how you arrived at your figures, or of any amounts that have been lumped together under one heading such as 'other payments'. A well-informed reader will be a happy reader, satisfied that you have given real consideration to the financial side of your business plan.

Your assumptions regarding debtor and creditor days should be fully explained. It could be useful to do a 'sensitivity analysis'. For example, if your sales forecast was to be reduced by 10 per cent, what effect would this have on your cash? How much each month, and for the whole year?

UNDERSTANDING YOUR BALANCE SHEET

Your balance sheet is an overview showing the financial position of your business at a specific time. It generally shows the position at the year end, but during your initial trading period it is advisable to produce one at least once a quarter to help you analyse how well you are performing. This analysis can then be used to make any necessary amendments to your business strategy in order to maintain or improve upon your current trading position.

In simple terms a balance sheet forecast will be a forecast of both your assets and liabilities. Your assets will include everything that your business actually owns; your liabilities will include all the money your business owes. Assets can then be further divided into fixed and current assets, and liabilities into short- and long-term liabilities. A fixed asset will remain a part of the business for a long period of time (*eg* a building or vehicle). A current asset will only remain with the business for a short term (*eg* raw materials, stock).

Your balance sheet will help you understand where all of the money that has come into your business has come from and where it has gone.

Balance sheet forecast for 31 December 200X

	£	£
Fixed assets		56,213
Current assets		
Raw materials	15,914	
Stock in hand	27,548	
Debtors	10,351	
Cash in the bank	11,785	
Total current assets	65,598	
Current liabilities		
Creditors	8,656	
Tax liability	1,618	
Overdraft	2,549	
Total liabilities	12,823	
Net current assets (Working capital)		52,775
Net assets		108,988
Financed by		
Owner's investment	45,000	
Bank loans	40,000	
Retained profit	23,988	
Total capital		108,988

Fig. 5. Example of a balance sheet.

PRODUCING YOUR BALANCE SHEET

Most of the financial data to be included in your balance sheet will be extracted from your profit and loss and cashflow forecasts. Much of the work has already been completed, so your next task is to extract the necessary information to complete your forecast both accurately and professionally.

Figure 5 shows a typical balance sheet forecast which will be referred to during this section. The first half of your balance sheet will show where your capital of £108,988 has been distributed among the various assets you have obtained; the second half where it came from.

Fixed assets

These are permanent items such as buildings, land, machinery, vehicles and plant which will be used in your business for a long period of time. In normal economic conditions, you should calculate and adjust their current worth by allowing for **appreciation** in case of buildings and land, and **depreciation** when valuing your machinery, vehicles and plant. If you can spare the resources, it is a good idea to start putting cash aside to cover the eventual replacement costs of your depreciating assets.

Current assets

These are items held for a short period of time before being converted into an item which can be sold. A raw material is an example of a current asset; it is bought in and then assembled into a finished product before being sold and eventually paid for. Raw materials, finished stock, debtors and any cash would all be included as your current assets.

Current liabilities

Your current liabilities are calculated by adding together all of your temporary debts which will be repaid within a short period of time, generally no more than 12 months. These liabilities will include all debts to your creditors (suppliers), the bank for your overdraft, and interest on any loans in addition to any outstanding tax and VAT payments.

Net current assets

This is more commonly referred to as **working capital**. It is calculated by subtracting all of your current liabilities from the total of your current assets. If your current liabilities exceed your current assets then this section will become your net current liabilities; in other words your business will owe more money than it has available. You would be running a serious risk of 'trading while knowingly insolvent' or even bankruptcy.

Net assets

Your net assets are worked out by adding together the totals of both your fixed assets and net current assets (working capital).

Financed by

This section shows where the capital has come from in order to finance your assets. It will include any capital investment made by yourself and any long-term loans from banks or other financial institutions. You will also need to include the total profit or loss for the accounting period to which the balance sheet relates. This information can easily be extracted from your profit and loss forecast.

Tidying it all up

In order for your balance sheet to be accurate the total of your net assets must be equal to the total of the capital that has been introduced. If it is not, you will have to go back over your totals and re-calculate your figures until the two totals do balance.

Any items that require further clarification should be included in your accompanying supplementary notes. However, remember that most of these totals would have been explained with your profit and loss and cashflow forecasts and you should not need to repeat any of your comments.

BREAKING EVEN

Your potential backers or investors will be interested to see that your business is forecast to generate a profit. Every business has a **break-even point**, the point at which the total sales revenue is equal to the total costs. In simple terms any amount below this point represents a loss and anything above means a profit.

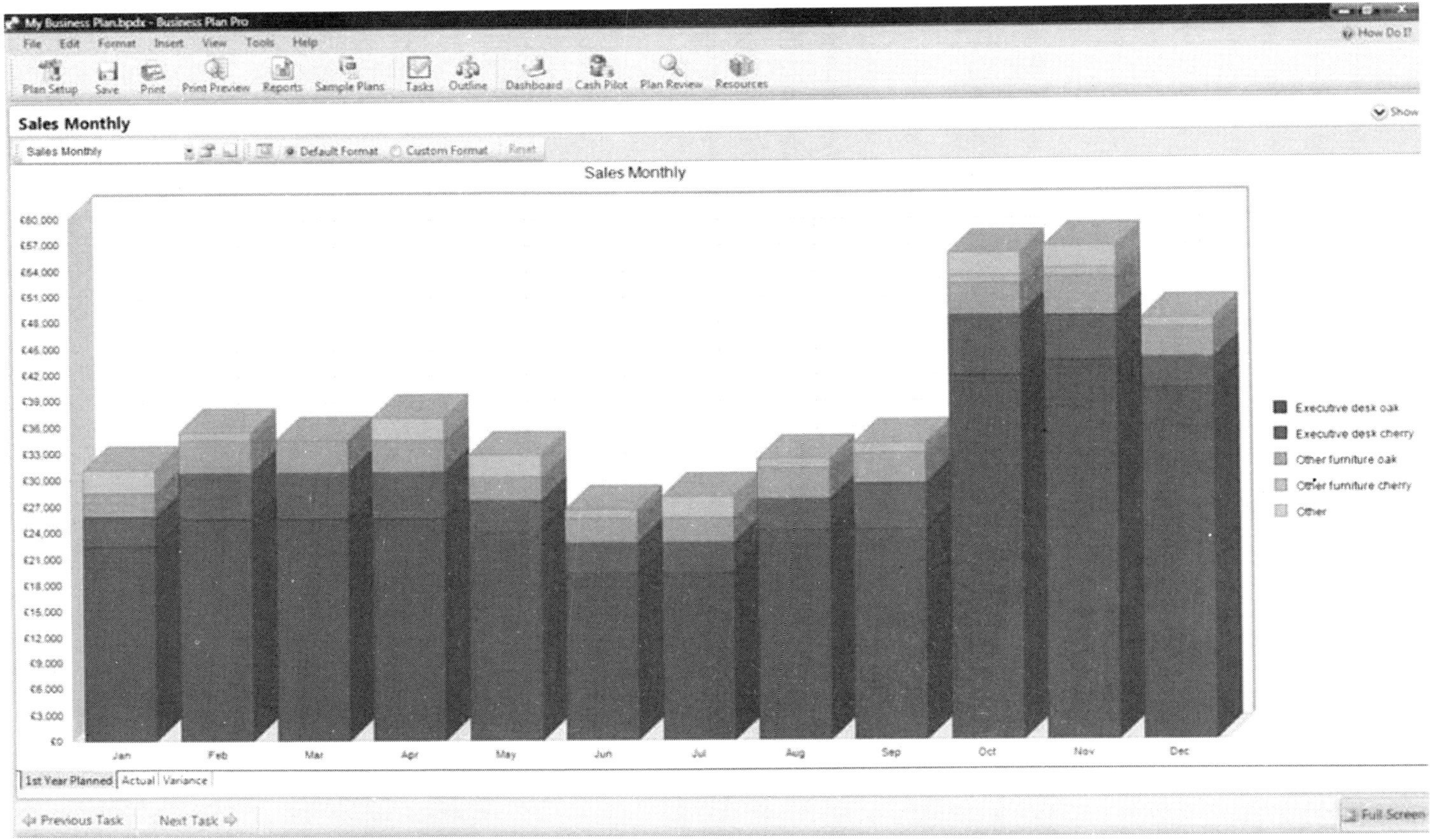

Fig. 6. Screenshot from Business Planning Pro by PaloAlto Software.

The nature of your business will determine how you measure your break-even point. For example, if your business involves producing or assembling a finished product, the break-even point will be expressed as the amount of units that need to be sold to cover your costs. However, if you are offering a service then you need to ascertain how many paid hours you need to work to cover your costs.

Alternative methods of financial forecasting

A variety of software packages is available to help with your financial planning but as single, stand-alone programs, these can be quite expensive. As a cheaper alternative, consider using an integrated forecast tool built into some of the more comprehensive business planning software programs. For example, *Business Planning Pro* by PaloAlto Software has an excellent forecast tool that allows you to type numbers directly into cells, draw a graphic forecast with your mouse, or apply a growth rate percentage. By default, tables in the main business plan are automatically calculated and printed as yearly totals with monthly first year figures included within the appendix. Information can be either through a guided wizard or a spreadsheet formula and powerful help tools are embedded within the program to assist with the completion of your business plan.

We are delighted to offer our readers a special 20 per cent discount on *Business Plan Pro* (RRP £79.99) and *Business Plan Pro Premier* (RRP £129.99). To order please call 0845 351 9924 and mention this offer. For more information visit www.paloalto.co.uk or www.bplans.co.uk where you will find extensive free business planning resources that have been compiled by PaloAlto.

CHECKLIST

- What evidence do you have to support your sales projection?
- Have you devised a contingency plan in case your financial projections do not go according to plan?
- What is the difference between a cashflow forecast, and a profit and loss forecast?
- Have you compiled your cashflow forecast?

- Does your profit and loss forecast indicate that your business venture will be viable?
- Have you produced a balance sheet to show your financial position the day before you begin trading?
- What is your projected break-even point? What level of sales are needed to achieve this?
- Will your clients expect you to provide them with credit? If so, have you devised a system of credit control to monitor their payments?

CASE STUDIES

Joshua and Jake prepare their second business plan

As the first bank they visited did not even suggest the Small Firms Loan Guarantee (SFLG) scheme, Joshua and Jake decided to take their proposal to another bank. Presenting their proposal on a rival bank's stationery would do little to enhance their chances of approval, so a second plan had to be put together. If only they had considered compiling their own business plan in the first place all this extra work could have been easily avoided.

After many more long nights the document was completed and sent to the bank with an accompanying letter. This would give the bank manager time to familiarise himself with their proposal before they all met.

Jasmine needs to expand

Business has been going so well for Jasmine that the time has come to expand. Calendar Creations has outgrown the office workshop set up in one of her spare bedrooms. A small industrial unit is now needed and at least one full-time and one part-time member of staff if the business is to continue to grow and develop at its current rate. Jasmine could just afford these development costs herself but she feels it would leave her in a very vulnerable financial position. Instead she decides to approach her bank for additional finance in the form of a business development loan.

Luke applies for a relocation grant

With his business plan compiled, Luke went before the grant board and presented his case. Due to the nature of his business and the fact that he would be creating an additional 20 jobs, the board looked favourably on his application, although it was a further three months before the £200,000 relocation grant and £100,000 subsidised loan was finally approved and made available to him. Luke could now expand his business and meet the demands of the extra workloads created by his new contract which had also boosted his business in general by enabling his business to become internationally known.

Action points

1. Consider what steps you can take to improve your cashflow if your sales revenue does not meet your expectations.
2. Looking at your profit and loss forecast, what methods can you use to increase the profitability of your business?
3. Consider the effect on your business if the cost price of your product or service were to dramatically increase. Could this cost be absorbed in your business or would you have to increase your selling price? How would this affect your position in the market place? Do you think your clients would still be prepared to pay the new price?

7

Your Financial Analysis

Unless you are one of the few people with plenty of savings or capital to finance your business yourself then the chances are that you will be looking for further financial assistance. Many of the businesses launched without the further need to borrow go on to become highly successful and prosperous. However even these businesses may need to borrow at a later date as they expand and develop.

If you do need to borrow any more money it is important to be well prepared before seeking any outside help.

SPECIFYING YOUR FINANCIAL NEEDS

Three key questions

The financial analysis of your business plan should lead you to the answers of the following questions:

- How much money do you need and exactly what will you need it for?
- What type of finance do you need and when will you need it?
- How will the money be repaid, and how will your investors or backers benefit from their investment?

This chapter will help you answer the above questions which will have to be answered in your business plan.

PLANNING YOUR BORROWING

Your cashflow and balance sheet forecasts will be invaluable tools when you are planning how much money you will need and what it will be used for. Even though your forecasts will not be a true picture of exactly how your financial year will develop, they will act as a very good indicator (provided your research is accurate). Your cashflow forecast will show the available funds you will have access to at any one time, assuming you achieve your expected level of sales and your overheads do not exceed your forecast.

Your reader will not have the time to work out how much money you will need and what it will be used for so you will have to supply this information in the simplest way possible. The best way to do this is to draw up a **financial requirement statement**. This will summarise how much money you need and quickly show your reader what it will be used for.

Example financial requirement statement

A net investment of £200,000 will be needed which will be distributed in the following way:

The money will be used to purchase:	£
Premises	75,000
Plant	10,000
Equipment	15,000
It will provide:	
Working capital for the first 12 months of trading	150,000
Total capital investment	250,000
Less personal investment	(50,000)
Total net funding	200,000

Every financial statement you make in your business plan must be supported with evidence that the figures you have presented are correct. Your balance sheet can be used to support the totals of your fixed assets; your cashflow forecast will provide the necessary evidence for your working capital needs. Once again, remember that these figures have already been substantiated with your forecast so just a reference to these documents will be sufficient. However, ensure that the money you say you need matches the figures in your forecasts.

There is a very fine line between borrowing too much finance and not borrowing enough. Too much means that it will cost you more than you really have to pay, whilst too little will mean going back to your lender at a later stage, and he will not look favourably on your request if your initial projections were way out.

UNDERSTANDING THE VARIOUS TYPES OF FINANCE

The length of time you require your finance to last will depend on which of the many different types of finance will best suit you and your business. There are traditionally four types of finance:

- permanent;
- long-term;
- medium-term;
- short-term.

Permanent finance

If your business is as a sole trader or partnership the permanent finance would come in the form of the capital you or your partners personally put in, plus any profits that have been made and retained in your business. However, if you intend to launch as, or develop into, a limited company then your permanent finance will be structured slightly differently: it will come from the sale of shares, including perhaps investment from venture capital organisations. This method of permanent finance will usually mean that the investor will expect to either receive a percentage of ownership or have some control over your profits.

However, on the positive side, this finance can be used to buy virtually anything needed for the business such as fixed and current assets, and used as a cash reserve against unforeseen expenses.

Long-term finance

This type of finance will be borrowed from external sources over a long period of time, usually anywhere between five and 25 years. A commercial mortgage or long-term loan agreement from one of the main clearing banks are examples of long-term finance. The money can be used for any long-term assets such as your business premises and any expensive machinery or plant.

Medium-term finance

Any borrowing that will be repaid over a 2–7 year period can be described as medium-term finance. This finance is commonly based on an agreement between yourself and the organisation who will be providing it. It will cover:

- hire purchase;
- leasing;
- loan agreements.

Short-term finance

The most typical and frequently used type of short-term finance is the bank overdraft facility. Although the **arrangement fees** can be fairly hefty you have the advantage of only paying interest on the amount you are actually overdrawn. With a bank loan, on the other hand, you have the use of a set amount of money and will pay interest whether you use the full amount or not.

If your business experiences seasonal trends and you need extra finance to cover stock purchases then an overdraft will be the ideal way to finance them; you will soon reduce the overdraft again when your seasonal rush gets underway.

The credit you receive from your suppliers is not often referred to as a form of finance, but whenever you are able to obtain and use goods before any payment is made then this is still a type of finance.

TIMING YOUR FINANCE

Having examined the various finance options open to you, what you need it for will have the biggest influence on which method you choose. When you have decided how much money you need and why, you should be able to manage things so that not all of the money will be needed at once. For example, the capital you need to acquire your premises or equipment will probably be required weeks, if not months, before you start trading. On the other hand your working capital will not be needed until you start trading.

ASSESSING OTHER SOURCES OF FINANCE

Most businesses look towards the main clearing banks to raise the necessary finance but if for whatever reason this avenue fails then there are many other less conventional methods to choose between. If the bank has turned down your application for finance then ask yourself why. Maybe your business is not quite the viable proposition that you consider it to be. However, many propositions have initially been turned down by one or more banks, but have gone on to become highly successful business ventures. Anita Roddick of Body Shop fame is just one example. Here are a few examples of other sources of finance:

Raising venture capital

Venture capital companies

Unless you are either a well established business or looking to raise £250,000 or more, few venture capital companies will be interested in the opportunity that you are offering.

Business angels

The alternative for new business start-ups is private investment by way of informal equity capital. Informal equity capital is put up by so-called 'business angels'. Business angels operate much like venture capital companies. They are considered to be the first step to obtaining corporate venture capital later on as your business grows and needs extra investment for development and expansion.

Both types of business will require a comprehensive business plan which will show not only detailed financial projections but also the complete background of your management team, and information regarding your potential investors' return on their investment.

The Enterprise Investment Scheme

The government offers various tax relief advantages for investors through the Enterprise Investment Scheme (EIS). This replaced the Business Expansion Scheme in January 1994. Further information about this scheme can be obtained from the Enterprise Investment Scheme Association at Erico House, 93–99 Upper Richmond Road, London SW15 2TG. Tel: 020 8785 5560. Fax: 020 8785 5561. Email: members@eisa.org.uk Website: www.eisa.org.uk

Business contacts

A full listing of companies specialising in raising informal equity capital can be obtained from the **British Venture Capital Association** (BVCA) at 3 Clements Inn, London WC2A 2AZ. Tel: 020 7025 2950. Email: bvca@bvca.co.uk Website: bvca.co.uk The BVCA represents virtually every major source of venture capital in the UK. Its members include venture capital firms, professional advisers, corporate financiers, mezzanine firms and other companies whose executives are experienced in the venture capital field. The BVCA's primary objective is to increase awareness and general perception of venture capital.

Accountants, stockbrokers and solicitors are an excellent source of information as these organisations have direct contact with a large number of clients who may be able to offer you investment for your venture. Further help and advice about the venture capital process can be obtained from your local Business Link operator. To find your local office, either visit www.businesslink.gov.uk or telephone 0845 600 9 006.

Applying for government assistance

Contrary to public belief, the government is taking positive steps to assist business and industry as a whole although this may not always appear to be the case. There are currently millions of pounds set aside for the sole purpose of providing various grants and government-subsidised loans in a bid to encourage investment and development. In general the government is looking to assist projects which benefit areas of declining industries with high levels of unemployment, as well as promoting growth and improvement in under-developed urban and rural areas.

Further help and advice about applying for, and obtaining, grants can be obtained from your local Business Link operator. To find your local office, either visit www.businesslink.gov.uk or telephone 0845 600 9 006.

Small Firms Loan Guarantee (SFLG) scheme

If you have a viable business proposition but lack the necessary security to obtain a loan, then the Small Firms Loan Guarantee (SFLG) may be the answer. The SFLG is a joint venture between the Department for Business, Enterprise & Regulatory Reform (BERR) and a variety of participating lenders. The scheme provides lenders with a government-backed guarantee covering 75 per cent of the loan amount, for which the borrower pays a two per cent premium to the BERR on the outstanding balance. Under the scheme, loans of up to £250,000 are available with repayment terms of up to 10 years.

Further information about the SFLG and participating lenders can be obtained from the Ministerial Correspondence Unit, Department for Business, Enterprise and Regulatory Reform, 1 Victoria Street, London SW1H 0ET. Tel: 020 7215 5000. Fax: 020 7215 0105. Email: enquiries@berr.gsi.gov.uk Website: www.berr.gov.uk

Offering your shares to the public

If your business is a well established limited company, then you could consider raising capital by offering your shares to the public. A full listing on the stock exchange will be very costly and probably a long way off for your business at present. However there is now a more relaxed option available through the **Alternative Investment Market** (AIM) which is operated, regulated and promoted by the London Stock Exchange. It was set up to replace the Unlisted Securities Market (USM) and since its launch in 1995 over 2,500 companies have joined the AIM and collectively raised over £34bn. AIM is open to all companies regardless of their country of origin. Although this represents an easier route to offering your shares to the general public, it is still a very complex process which should only be undertaken after seeking professional advice from your accountant.

For further information about the Alternative Investment Market contact London Stock Exchange, 10 Paternoster Square, London EC4M 7LS. Tel: 020 7797 1000. Website: www.londonstockexchange.com

The Prince's Trust

The Prince's Trust is a UK charity that runs a range of programmes to help, support and advise young people. Of particular note is the Business Programme which can provide low interest loans of up to £4,000 (up to £5,000 for partnerships), ongoing advice from a business mentor, access to a wide range of products services, grants of up to £1,500 and test marketing grants of up to £250. To be eligible you must be between 18 and 30 and either unemployed or working fewer than 16 hours a week.

For further information contact The Prince's Trust, 18 Park Square East, London NW1 4LH. Tel: 020 7543 1234. Fax: 020 7543 1200. Email: webinfops@princes-trust.org.uk Website: www.princes-trust.org.uk

Raising private loans

There may be friends, relatives or colleagues who are in a position to lend you money. Although it may seem like a good idea at the time, you can almost guarantee that they will demand their money back when you can least afford it. Therefore it is important to get the terms of the loan written down clearly and precisely in order to avoid any confusion at a later date. The points you should cover include details of:

- the final date of repayment;
- the frequency and amount of interim repayments;
- any rate of interest, and the date when due;
- whether the loan will entitle the lender to any control over the business.

Approaching finance houses

These companies may be able to provide you with finance but they are mainly secondary lenders. This means that the money they lend to you has been borrowed by themselves in the first instance. Therefore your repayments will not only have to cover the cost of your lenders' borrowing but also allow the lender to make a profit. This is why finance houses tend to be an expensive option. Advertisements for these companies can be found in most national newspapers. If you consider this option, never sign any documents unless you are completely sure of all the contractual terms and you have first taken the professional advice of your own solicitor or accountant. There are many unscrupulous companies within this industry so make sure they are registered as a **Member of the Corporation of Finance Brokers**.

Cash from factoring

If you begin to experience cashflow problems, it may be because much of your capital is tied up with debtors in the form of overdue invoices. There may a solution to this situation. Factoring is a method many businesses use to turn unsettled invoices into immediate working capital. The idea is very simple. You would forward details of your outstanding invoices to the factoring company and in return they will advance you up to 80 per cent of the value of these invoices. The other 20 per cent will be received as and when your client finally settles their invoice (less a certain fee which will be retained by the factoring company for providing this facility in the first instance). In addition to this, factoring companies can also maintain your sales ledgers, offer a credit control and collection service, assess credit risks and provide insurance against bad debts.

Your bank manager or accountant will be able to recommend a good factoring company. The Asset Based Finance Association (ABFA) is the regulatory body set up to keep tight control over the factoring industry. ABFA can be contacted at Boston House, The Little Green, Richmond, Surrey TW9 1QE. Tel: 020 8332 9955. Fax: 020 8332 2585. Website: abfa.org.uk

RAISING YOUR FINANCE

Having decided the amount and type of finance you require, your next task is to actually raise the necessary funds. By examining the two previous sections you will have a better understanding about whom to approach for your finance. This section of your business plan must be tailor-made to suit your particular lender or investor. Telling your reader about how you intend to repay the money you wish to borrow and then presenting your business plan to an investor instead of a lender will do little to generate any faith in your business venture.

Approaching lenders

Unless your potential lenders have taken leave of their senses they will not be prepared to lend you any money if they have any doubt that your business will generate enough profit and cash to meet the repayments. Your cashflow and profit and loss forecasts should be referred to when illustrating how and when you will be able to make repayments of your loan.

Putting up security

Whether you approach one of the main clearing banks or any other financial institution you must firstly include details of any security you have to support your loan application. This could be in the form of:

- personal savings in addition to the capital investment you are already making;
- any equity you have built up within your home;
- details of any life assurance and endowment policies.

You must be able to prove that the amount of security you are offering is correct. Making a glib estimate about the value of equity in your home will not be enough on its own. You must support this with a letter from your estate agent, surveyor or valuer stating the value of your property. Copies of your mortgage documents and any policies are also ideal and must be included in your appendices alongside the estate agent's letter.

Think long and hard before you offer security of this nature. Will you be prepared to surrender this in the event of things going wrong?

Persuading potential investors

When describing your financial requirements to your potential investors, you must not just show that you have a viable business opportunity but also describe how *they* will be able to directly benefit from their investment. The deal you are offering must be attractive to them. You must be able to hold their interest long enough for them to consider taking your proposition one step further by investing their money.

In exchange for a capital investment most offers would typically include a percentage of ownership. This in turn would give your investor a limited amount of control within the business and a share of any profits equal to the value of their percentage of ownership. This would probably be in the form of dividends. Although your lenders may be prepared to wait a long time for their loan to be repaid, your investors may not be quite so patient to see a return on their money. Therefore, when you make your offer it is important that your potential investor is made aware of how they are able to **exit** from your business if they choose to.

Exit clauses

An exit clause must be offered but you may decide to put a minimum time limit of perhaps five years or longer before they are able to relinquish their interest in your business. However if they choose to sell out then you could suggest they sell their interest back to you at a pre-agreed price per share, or to a mutually acceptable third party. Whichever method you choose ensure that you have a draft agreement drawn up and include it within your appendices.

CHECKLIST

- Have you carefully calculated how much money you will require to get your business established?
- Have you produced a breakdown of this figure?
- Do you know what source of finance you will use to raise the necessary capital?
- Have you calculated exactly when you will need the finance that you are looking for?
- Have you made a list of your preferred lenders?

- Have you explained how and when your backers will be repaid and how your investors can benefit from the investment they have made?
- Can your business support the level of borrowing needed to get it launched?
- Have you considered taking any legal advice and has this actually been done?
- Have you compiled a financial statement which shows where you expect the necessary capital to come from and exactly how it will be used?
- Do you know if you are eligible for any government grants or subsidised loans which may be available?

CASE STUDIES

Joshua and Jake visit another bank

By now Joshua and Jake knew their business inside out and were completely prepared for every eventuality that this meeting may present. The meeting went very well and their suggestion to use the Small Firms Loan Guarantee (SFLG) scheme to overcome their lack of security was warmly received.

All proposals for the scheme must be supported with a recommendation from a bank. Although the final approval must come from the offices of the scheme, this is generally only a formality. After a long uphill struggle Joshua and Jake were finally within reach of running their own business.

Jasmine prepares her second business plan

Although Jasmine's first business plan was prepared for her own benefit, it did provide her with the necessary skills and experience to produce a professionally presented business plan – essential if she was to get the loan to assist with her expansion plans. Jasmine's business plan would be based on the information contained in her first plan with any necessary facts and figures updated. Her financial projections for Calendar Creations were likely to be more accurate now the forecast could be based on a combination of actual trading figures and orders received, rather than the pure estimates of her original business plan.

Jasmine's business plan would show how the loan would be used to further develop her current level of service by introducing a range of calendars and diaries that could not only be personalised with important dates but also with the clients' own photographs. This new range would make excellent presents and business gifts. Although there would be an additional 50 per cent increase on the selling price, market research indicated that her clients would be prepared to pay it.

Luke finds a private investor

Until the government relocation grant and subsidised loan had been approved, Luke found tremendous difficulty in getting potential investors to commit themselves to his business opportunity. Many private investors expressed an interest but until the government approval was obtained they were reluctant to invest their money. However, now that the government had made its commitment a private investor was quickly found and the business could now begin to operate at full production following the purchase of the much needed additional machinery.

Action points

1. List the different methods of raising finance that are available to you. What are the advantages and disadvantages of the type that you have selected to finance your business?
2. If you were to offer an outside investor shares in your business in exchange for cash, what effect could this have on how you decide to control your business?
3. Consider which methods you will use to determine exactly how much capital you require to launch your business.

8

Adding Your Appendices

The appendices will be the last section of your business plan to be compiled, but not until the rest of your plan has been written will you be able to do so. The appendices are a collection of documents, illustrations, samples and literature which will help to reinforce and substantiate all of the comments and assumptions you have made. Without any documentary evidence to back up your business plan it is unlikely you will convince potential backers to provide any kind of finance.

WHAT TO INCLUDE IN YOUR APPENDICES

Even though each and every business plan will vary in content there are a number of different headings which will be apparent in nearly all business plans. Under each of these headings are examples of the documents which can be included within the appendices:

The nature of the business

- A map of your location in relation to your competition and to your intended market.
- Any relevant media reports from newspapers or magazines.
- Written details of correspondence from your professional advisers such as an accountant, solicitor or surveyor.
- An agreement showing the freehold or leasing details of your premises.
- Details of any trading history to date. This will obviously only apply if you are buying an already established business. A summary of the previous three years will be sufficient.

Key personnel

- Full curricula vitae for all the key members of your management team.
- Any certificates or diplomas awarded to any of your personnel. The originals will carry far more weight than photocopies.
- Details of any partnerships or incorporation agreement.
- An organisation chart showing who will be responsible for each department.

Your market

- Details of any firm orders, and previous client sales records.
- Relevant newspaper or magazine articles with details about your market.
- Details of any outside help from trade associations, chamber of commerce, business links or the government.
- Details of market research methods and results.
- Any information about your competitors such as their prices and details about their premises.

Products and services

- Price lists from your suppliers and the competition.
- Details of product lead times.
- Any independent reports from consultants and the media.
- Details of your sales literature, promotional and advertising material.
- Applications for copyright, design and patents.

Financial

- Cashflow forecasts.
- Profit and loss statement.
- Balance sheet.

- Estimates for your overheads.
- Proof of your capital contributions such as bank statements or any policies you may have.

POSITIONING YOUR APPENDICES

Where to position your appendices will largely depend on how many supportive documents you intend to include, and how many pages they will span. If you will only be using a modest amount then it will be best to put them all at the end. This will keep your business plan as a single document and will let the recipient read through your plan as if it is a book. However, if your appendices number too many to fit easily within your plan then it will look more professional to produce a secondary file and clearly mark it 'Appendices'.

In order to continue the high level of professionalism you have so far created and developed, ensure your appendices file is the same colour, style, make and design as the ones you have chosen for your business plan. If your appendices are to be included in a second file then make sure this is made clear on the contents page of your business plan. Just a footnote referring to the second file will be sufficient, *eg* 'Appendices are in the accompanying file'.

When you send your business plan to your bank manager or potential investor it is unlikely the intended recipient will be the actual person who will open your letter and business plan. In most cases it will be a secretary or a member of their staff. Since your business plan should arrive at least a few days before your meeting then the chances are it will be put on a desk or a shelf until the day. During this time the possibility of two files finding their way onto different desks or shelves is quite high. By bringing the reader's attention at the beginning to the fact that there should be two files will avoid any confusion at a later stage. Before the reader assumes that you have forgotten to include the appendices in your file, the footnote will indicate a file is missing.

PRESENTING YOUR APPENDICES

You have now decided where your appendices will be positioned in relation to your business plan and which ones you intend to use. Consider next how to present these documents in such a way that the reader will want to study them. This in turn will lead to a greater understanding of your business plan.

The supportive documents which will make up your appendices come in all shapes and sizes but there are only two sources these can come from:

1. documents produced and compiled by yourself and your colleagues; or
2. documents supplied by outside sources such as estate agents, accountants and surveyors.

It does not matter where your appendices have come from, they will all end up in the same file at the end of your business plan. Therefore no matter how different in appearance they are, they must all look uniform and as though they belong together in the same file.

Internally compiled documents

Documents compiled by yourself or colleagues are much more fun to work with. They can be altered or changed as many times as you wish before your finished document has been fully compiled. The only two rules to abide by are:

- do not distort the truth;
- do not amend the information for your own benefit.

This will only mislead the reader, and when you are found out the reader will assume you to be a poor business person with little regard for honesty and integrity: not the best way to begin any working relationship.

A document checklist

There are many documents you may want to include yourself. These include:

- A map showing your premises in relation to the competition.
- An overhead view of your premises showing office space, working areas, fire escapes and so on.
- A curriculum vitae for each of the key members of your management team.

- A graph showing your proposed management structure and if necessary the position of your potential investors.
- Results of any market research studies you have conducted.

Externally provided documents

The dangers of 'doctoring'

Documents provided by external sources should be left just the way they are. Any attempt to 'improve' the quality or layout of these documents by correcting spelling mistakes, doctoring photocopies or re-writing text will only undermine their authenticity. Wherever possible try to provide the original document unless it is either very valuable or difficult to replace. If a photocopy is used, make sure you have the original with you at your meeting.

Highlighting key points

Despite not being able to change the appearance of these documents, there are a number of ways you can make your appendices more appealing to the reader. To begin with, read through them as though you were to be the recipient of your business plan, and ask yourself if all the information you are presenting is really necessary. The key points you want to get across may well be buried in paragraphs of text. A simple fluorescent highlighting pen will help bring the reader's attention directly to the key points.

Adding notes

For graphs, reports or newspaper extracts, a short explanatory note at the bottom of the document or details of when and where the newspaper article was published, will help the reader to understand why you have included these appendices.

COMPILING YOUR APPENDICES

Now that you have an idea about what information needs to be included in the appendices, your next task is to put them into an order that will enable the reader to be able to quickly refer to them. The compiling of your appendices should coincide with the final editing of your business plan. Begin by putting all of the documentary evidence that you have so far collated in a pile in front of you. Along with this pile you will also need your business plan and a blank piece of paper.

1. Start by carefully reading through your business plan page by page.
2. At every point where a reference is made to a fact, figure or statistic, make a note of it on your blank piece of paper.
3. Try to find a document from your pile of appendices to substantiate these comments.
4. This formerly blank piece of paper will now form the basis for the contents page of your appendices.

When you have finished reading through your business plan you may find that you have a few documents which still remain without a home. If this is the case, read back over the text with these documents in the front of your mind and try to build them into your plan remembering also to list them in the contents page.

NUMBERING YOUR APPENDICES

With all of your comments backed up by documentary evidence, the next step is to make sure the reader is able to refer to them with ease. This can be done simply by numbering each appendix and using that same number in the text of your business plan. Your appendices should now follow the same order as the notes you have made on your piece of paper.

Begin by numbering the first document Appendix 1, then Appendix 2, Appendix 3 and so on. Try to resist using the number system 1.1, 1.2, 1.3 and so on for any multiple page appendices such as audited accounts for example. This will only make the task of finding an appendix more difficult to the reader and will make your contents page look cluttered.

Completing the contents page

Now that your appendices are all individually numbered, the appendices contents page can now be compiled. Begin by numerically listing the appendices down the left side of the page following with a brief description of each one. For example:

Appendix 1:	Town map showing the position of the business in relation to the competition.
Appendix 2:	Market research results showing a definite need for our service.

Down the right side of the page list the page numbers which relate to the appendices. This will now form the layout for the contents page of your appendices and help the reader to quickly refer to a particular section.

CHECKLIST

- Have you selected which information you will include in your appendices?
- Has the information been fully numbered and catalogued for easy reference by your reader?
- Have you referred to your appendices in the text of your business plan?
- Do you know where your appendices will appear within your business plan?
- Have you presented all of your information in a uniform style to give it the impression of fitting together?
- Have you highlighted the relevant text of the lengthier documents so that the reader's attention is immediately drawn to key facts, figures and data?

CASE STUDIES

Joshua and Jake sign the contracts

When the loan was finally approved, all that remained was for the contracts to be signed and exchanged. Even though this was a tried and tested franchise concept, and the contract had been used and approved on many previous occasions, Joshua and Jake decided to take legal advice and appointed a solicitor to read through the document prior to signing. The solicitor did not find any reason to delay signing, so the contracts were exchanged and the business was finally theirs.

Jasmine visits the bank

Jasmine's business plan was sent to the bank long before her meeting with the bank manager. Based on her previous trading history and her plans to develop new product lines such as the personalised organisers, the bank did not hesitate in lending her the £7,000 required to finance extra equipment, employ staff and move into new premises. Her loan was secured on the £10,000 balance she had managed to accumulate in her business account.

Luke's business prospers

Luke's business began to prosper as production levels reached an all time high. In just 18 months following the introduction of the new contract his sales revenue had increased to just under £3 million. Both the grant board and private investor were encouraged by the level of production and turnover being so good.

However, coping with the extra workload had resulted in the business gradually monopolising more and more of Luke's time. In turn, this had led to the fundamental aspects of running a business being ignored. Too much time and energy was being spent ensuring that all deadlines were met and not enough time given to controlling the basics such as expenditure and employing the right members of staff.

Action points

1. Are the assumptions or important information you have written about during the business plan supported with any additional evidence?
2. Devise a uniform method of presenting your information.
3. During the course of compiling your business plan you will collate a large amount of additional information. Determine which information to include and which to disregard.

9

Presenting Your Plan

By the time you have finished compiling your business plan you will have invested a great deal of time and energy. You will have ensured that all the information you have presented is both accurate and of a quality second to none. However, unless you present your business plan effectively all this hard work may be wasted.

COMPOSING YOUR INTRODUCTORY LETTER

When you attend an interview for a job or meet someone for the first time you want to make a good first impression. It is this first impression that people will always remember. The same can be said for a business plan; how a potential investor first becomes aware of your business idea will be how they will remember it and you.

An introductory letter will be the first point of contact your potential investors will have about you and your business idea. This should be sent at least seven days prior to your meeting and will serve as a brief introduction about you and your business. Time taken now to compile a professional letter of introduction will be time well spent. There are many different ways to write a good business letter and although there is no single specific right way there are many ways which look untidy and unprofessional.

All your business letters must be typed or if you are fortunate enough to have access to one, then use a word processor. Never under any circumstance write a business letter by hand. It gives the impression of an unorganised person with little interest in professional presentation. After all if you are unable to present yourself professionally, then how will you convince anyone to back you?

Where to start

Invest a little time and money in having your business stationery professionally designed and printed. There are a number of companies who specialise in producing business start-up packs in a wide selection of attractive type styles and layouts. This is an inexpensive way of giving yourself a truly professional image. How much stationery you need will obviously depend on the size of your business but a good start would be to order at least 200 of the following:

- letterheads (A4);
- business cards;
- compliment slips;
- envelopes (DL).

Where your letterhead is positioned will determine where you begin your letter. If you have not already had your business stationery printed then always start at the top right hand side of the page with your address and contact telephone number with dialling code. A contact telephone is very important and should always be included. If you do not have one then include the number of a colleague or relative but remember to tell them you have used their number or you may have some explaining to do. A line should be left before the date is inserted on the left hand side of the page, and two more before including the reader's name, position and company address. Then leave another two lines before starting with the word 'Dear......'. If you do not know the reader's name then find it out. Pay particular attention to the spelling of the name as an incorrectly spelt surname can be infuriating.

A letter addressed to a specific person will look more professional and personal than a letter starting with 'Dear Sir'. Even less professional is 'Dear Sir or Madam'; this will resemble a circular sent by a desperate business person to each and every financial institution and potential backer.

What to write

You may wish to give the letter a title now before beginning your main text. This should start with the word 'Re:', which is an abbreviation for 'Reference' and then the title, for example, your business name or perhaps the nature of your forthcoming meeting.

The main text of your letter should be clear, concise and to the point. Remember, this is only to introduce yourself and your business idea. Further details and information can be provided when you meet your investor face to face. Always ensure your letter is double spaced between paragraphs with generous margins. This will not only make your letter appealing to the eye but also easy to read.

As you have taken the time to discover the receiver's name then close your letter with the words 'Yours sincerely' followed by a large space, then your name and if appropriate your job title. If you intend to send anything with your letter of introduction the words 'enc', or 'enclosures' will follow next with a description of what you are enclosing. It may be necessary to enclose your actual business plan either with your letter of introduction or at a later date. The reasons for doing this include:

- to give your potential backer a chance to read through your business plan prior to your meeting;
- if your potential backer lives too far way to have the meeting face to face.

If you do enclose your business plan, always ensure you have at least one other copy. Never under any circumstance send your last copy.

After you have finished your letter read back over it, then read it again and again. If possible get a friend or colleague to read over it. This will not only help eliminate any spelling and grammatical errors, it will also give you a second opinion about the content. If the letter does not read or appear perfect then continue re-writing it until it does sound right.

Figure 7 shows a sample letter of introduction sent by Jasmine Jade when she approached the bank for a Calendar Creations business loan.

SUBMITTING YOUR PLAN

Who you send your business plan to can be just as important as what you say in

Calendar Creations

5 Norton Road, Dottington, Surrey SF8 4BJ
Telephone: (0123) 456789, Fax: (0123) 987654

October 23, 200X

Mr. J. L. Richards
The Manager
Euro Bank
Dottington
Surrey SF4 2CR

Dear Mr. Richards

I am in the process of establishing my own business compiling and producing personalised calendars for which I have discovered there is a new niche market.

My total start up costs including working capital are £2,800 of which I have £1,400 of my own savings. As I have had a current account with Euro Bank for the last eight years I am looking to the bank to assist with financing the remaining £1,400 as a business loan.

Please find enclosed a business plan for your attention prior to our meeting on 1 November, 200X. I trust this will meet with your approval and I look forward to our forthcoming meeting.

Yours sincerely

Jasmine Jade

enclosure: Calendar Creations Business Plan

Figure 7. A sample letter of introduction.

the plan and letter themselves. Obviously what you want your business plan to achieve will influence who you send it to. For example, if you are looking to raise finance to back your new business or business idea then in the main you will probably be approaching at least one of, if not all of the main clearing banks. However, if you intend to introduce a potential investor to your business idea by offering some kind of equity then your business plan will be aimed at venture capital organisations. There are a great many of these as described in Chapter 7, so the same careful research you have used in developing your business idea should also be used when choosing which organisation to approach. Some organisations will only back businesses within a specific sector such as engineering or computing; others will only look at propositions that require a minimum investment of £250,000 or even far more.

Leave the final editing of your business plan until you know exactly who your reader will be. This will allow you to include information you know your reader will be personally interested to learn. You may even be able to give the impression you have personalised your business plan just for one specific reader when in fact all you have done is to amend small sections to make it appear that way. A simple way to personalise your plan without altering lots of sections is to personalise just the front page. This will not only make the reader feel important but also indicate your professionalism.

EXPLAINING YOUR BUSINESS

Just as you know all there is to know about your business, your potential backers know all there is to know about their business, whether it be lending money, backing viable opportunities or approving grant applications. Somewhere in the middle has to come a mutual understanding: it is unlikely that just from reading your business plan your backer will gain a full working knowledge of how your business works and why it will be a success. Therefore just as layman terms were used when writing your plan, the same approach should be used when explaining your business. The fact your backer is now only sitting across a desk from you does not mean that they will understand geophysics just because you have explained it to them face to face. When you are explaining your business:

- keep your explanations simple;
- keep them short;
- keep them interesting.

Remember, an interested backer is more likely to favour your business plan than someone who feels they would have had more fun watching the BBC test card.

MAKING A WINNING PROPOSAL

When the time comes to present yourself before your bank manager, investor or backer, treat the meeting just as you would any interview.

1. Long before the meeting sit down and have a good think about any points you want to raise and then jot them down on a piece of paper. This will help you to focus on what you need to say and how you will say it.
2. Show your list to your family and colleagues and monitor their response. There is no better criticism than constructive criticism. They may even have some thoughts of their own that you had not considered.
3. If you can, act out a mock interview, with a friend or colleague being the bank manager and you as yourself. The expressions on the face of the bank manager will show just how convincing you were.

Preparing for your meeting

Aim to arrive early for your meeting. Try not to look too eager as your bank manager may take this as a sign of desperation. Five to 10 minutes will give you time to clarify any points in your head and a chance to compose and relax yourself.

What to wear to the meeting can also present some problems. If you are hoping to secure a loan then you do not want to look as if you already have an overflowing wallet by wearing a tailormade Giorgio Armani suit, nor indeed will scruffy jeans and a shirt with holes give the impression of a person capable of repaying any kind of loan let alone running a business. A standard suit will usually be quite sufficient.

Who will speak

If all the key members of your team have been fully involved with preparing and researching your business idea then you will have compiled a good solid business plan. Solutions to any problems that arise would have been quickly resolved by your team pulling together.

It may be appropriate for some or all of them to be present at your meeting, so appoint a main spokesperson before you go in. There is nothing more annoying to a bank manager than trying to listen to more than one person speaking at any one time. It also gives the impression of a disorganised team. If you cannot work as a team now, then how will you cope when your business gets off the ground?

The main spokesperson should not be the *only* spokesperson; make sure everyone is able to make their own contribution at some point during the interview. This shows the backer you are able to work well as a team and that teamwork will be a strong influence on the success of your business.

Be prepared

Visual aids can be used to emphasise particular points but do not be fooled into thinking these will impress your bank manager. They will only make parts of your plan easier to understand, nothing more. Your business plan must be able to withstand stringent scrutiny, and your bank manager will be the first to put this to the test.

Do not be alarmed if the bank manager asks a lot of questions about your plan. This can be a positive sign. It shows they have read through it and are willing to find out more by clarifying points they are unsure of. Be ready to answer any point raised but never just waffle on like a politician and hope that if you continue talking for long enough your backer will forget what the original question was. It may work in the House of Commons but in a closed office it will do little to convince anyone that you know your product and your market. Remember, the objective of an interview is to see whether you have considered every eventuality in the running of your business, so be prepared to defend your plan against criticism.

SHOPPING AROUND

You may be in the fortunate position of having your business plan approved by the first organisation who examined it. But never accept the first offer you are made. If your business idea is so commercially viable then finding another backer will not present too much of a problem. In fact you may find backers falling over themselves to get your business. However, in the real world the chances of this happening, although possible, are extremely low.

When a bank finally agrees to arrange a loan it does not mark the end of the planning process but simply the beginning. Banks are keen to offer many spin-off products associated with a business loan such as pensions, life assurance, business insurance and health insurance to name but a few. Investors like to put their clients through a series of hoops before deciding upon their fate.

The best strategy to employ is to make a list of all those lenders you would really prefer to do with business with. The first name on the list will probably be the bank manager of your local branch. Put the rest in order of preference and work through them until you secure the deal you want.

Being refused

Do not be alarmed if your business plan is not accepted by the first organisation you approach. The reason for refusal is the most important part of any research for the perfect business plan. Think of refusal as a chance to amend, adapt and change your business plan before you are in a position to approach another potential backer. If the next backer also refuses your plan then modify it again and again until you finally get it right.

However, it does not matter how many modifications you make, an unrealistic business idea will not be able to hide behind any amount of fancy words or professional presentation. You will be fooling no one but yourself if you keep trying to pass off a poor business idea as a commercially viable one. You will not impress your potential backers by dressing up mutton as lamb. You will be politely shown the door.

CHECKLIST

- Has the final editing of your business plan been finished before your letter of introduction has been compiled?
- Have you written your letter of introduction? Do you know which information to include?
- Do you know who to send your letter to? Have you spelt their name correctly?
- Does your business plan look professional in its presentation?
- Has your business plan been personalised for your reader?
- Do you know how to present yourself at your meeting and have you planned what you will say?
- If there is to be more than one of you present at the interview, has a main spokesperson been appointed?
- Remember to keep your explanations, answers and information simple, short and interesting.
- Do you know where your meeting will take place? Have you planned how you will get there on time?
- Are you fully prepared for your meeting? Are any visual aids ready to use?
- Have you considered any alternative lenders or investors if your business plan is initially rejected?
- Each time you use your business plan for another lender or investor then remember to ensure that it is in pristine condition. Any torn or dirty pages should be immediately replaced.

CASE STUDIES

Joshua and Jake's success

Joshua and Jake completed their first year of trading with a 25 per cent increase on the previous year's sales revenue. This, combined with only an additional 10 per cent increase on their overheads, puts them in a very strong financial position. Their initial overdraft to finance working capital has been repaid and they have managed to accumulate a few thousand pounds in reserve capital.

They put their success down to a combination of being in complete financial control and using their business plan to constantly monitor their progress. Having to compile quarterly management figures as a condition of the Small Firms Loan Guarantee (SFLG) scheme has helped them keep a tight control over their finances which in turn led to a cash reserve.

Jasmine develops her business nationally

Over the next two years Calendar Creations developed into a very successful venture with 60 per cent of the sales revenue coming from repeat business. Jasmine has decided that the time has come to further expand her business. She still operates from the same industrial unit with eight full-time members of staff, her business is thriving and looks set to continue. The local area is well served but there still remains a large untapped market with huge growth potential.

Jasmine considered opening additional offices around the country but decided that the capital investment would be too much of a financial commitment. Instead she settles on a method of sub-contracting out postal districts to a small army of sales agents. These agents are to be employed on a commission basis and, for every calendar sold, the agent would keep 20 per cent of the selling price. Jasmine's only overheads are to supply her agents with their own printed stationery and to meet them half way with their advertising costs, a small price to pay to achieve national recognition.

Luke begins to experience problems

Trying to run a business with inadequately trained staff is simply asking for trouble. With Luke spending so much of his time on the shop floor ensuring that quality levels were being maintained and production targets met, the sales office was being left to run itself. Without a good credit control system being implemented and controlled, invoice payments began to get overlooked and a severe cashflow problem developed.

The sales staff tried to remedy the situation – not by chasing outstanding debts as they should have done, but by beginning to invoice clients as soon as an order was placed. For a short while this seemed to have solved the problem but in reality the company was now buying raw materials to produce products they had already been paid for. The results of this meant that customers became unhappy, all the sales figures were wrong, and a false picture of the financial position of the business was being portrayed.

Action points

1. List the main strengths and weaknesses of your proposed venture. How will you overcome any negative comments by your potential backers or investors?
2. Decide who will be first to see your business plan, and why.
3. Although you will not be able to plan exactly how your meeting will go, you can prepare yourself for it. Rehearse your presentation in front of a friend or colleague and then gauge their response.

10

Running Your Business to Plan

This section of the book assumes that the business plan you have prepared has now successfully achieved the purpose for which it was designed. This could have been to raise additional finance, attract an investor, or simply organise your ideas to see if your venture is a viable proposition. Whatever your reasons for preparing a business plan, this chapter is intended to help you ensure your business remains both profitable and successful.

Monitoring Your Business

Following the launch of your new venture you will risk being so preoccupied with the day-to-day running of your business that you may easily overlook the fundamentals which will make your business successful. It is important periodically to take time out to monitor how well your business is performing. Any potential problems can then be identified early on and preventive action taken to rectify matters. The penalties for failing to do this can be severe.

A small gradual loss of business may not be noticeable on a day-to-day basis but when you start comparing weekly and monthly figures then tailing off can be clearly seen. Any loss must be quickly identified and tackled to stop it increasing further. If clients are no longer buying your products or using your service, then find out why.

A busy business person will probably be so engrossed in their own work that they may not even have noticed the arrival of a new competitor or a fall in the standard of their work. If you are a sole trader then you will probably be constantly fighting against the clock to get your work done and your money in the bank, but time spent monitoring your progress is invaluable. A partnership or limited company will be better able to assess its situation as many jobs can be delegated giving you time to concentrate on your progress.

Who to talk to

Your accountant or bank manager are examples of people to discuss your business with. They tend to have impartial views and a wealth of experience behind them. A problem you are facing today could be resolved after speaking with them tomorrow. In addition, your local Enterprise Agency or Business Link have trained personnel to help you with any problems as they arise. If they are not able to assist you directly, they will be able to recommend sources of further help. However, sometimes just talking through a problem is often enough to help you see the solution for yourself.

USING YOUR BUSINESS PLAN

Try not to fall into the same trap as many other businesses by disregarding your business plan as soon as you are up and running. One of the most important, yet frequently overlooked reasons why you compiled a business plan in the first place was to use it to continually monitor how your business is performing. Many businesses feel that the plan has served its purpose as soon as the loan has been approved or the doors to the office are open. On the contrary, it merely marks the beginning.

Your first two years

For at least the first two years it is a good idea to sit down at least once a month either on your own, with your bank manager or accountant and use your business plan to analyse how well your business is doing. This will help you spot any problems long before they arise and take the necessary actions to stop them developing any further. For example, a steady decline in profits or cashflow will not always be apparent during the early stages of your venture whilst you are concentrating on the day-to-day running of your business but your sales revenue and cashflow forecasts will soon highlight any shortfalls.

How well is your business performing?

Use your business plan to monitor your progress; don't hide behind your business trying to convince everyone, including yourself, that everything is just fine. This will help you to face up to any problems you may be experiencing. It is far better to address any problems at an early stage and work towards solving them, rather than trying to cover them up; the latter will only lead to ever increasing debt and even bankruptcy.

Obviously you want your business venture to succeed because you have invested so much time, energy and capital getting it from the drawing board and into reality. However, there may come a time when you will have to face up to the fact that your new business venture is not working. Using your business plan to continually analyse your position will enable you to try something else before you lose too much.

On a more positive note, using your business plan to assess your current position will soon show if you are doing better than you expected. If this is the case you will be able to budget for further growth. Success leads to more success.

MANAGING YOUR CASHFLOW

Keeping a tight control over your cashflow will enable your business to prosper and succeed. Remember, cash is king. Without it your business is in danger of failing. Suppliers need to be paid and costs need to be met. This money has to come from somewhere and the best place is from your business bank account, provided you have sufficient funds available.

Once you begin to trade you will be able to compare your original cashflow projections with your current cashflow position. Do this on a regular basis, and see how well (or badly) your business is performing. You may be doing better than expected and have a cash surplus that needs to be invested so that your money is working harder for you. However, you may be in a poor cashflow position whereby drastic action is needed before bankruptcy looms. Close, careful monitoring of your cashflow will highlight these areas long before they become critical.

If your actual sales totals are equal to your estimated figures and your clients have paid their invoices then you are unlikely to experience any cashflow problems. However, in real life this is seldom the case, but there are some precautions you can take which will help your cashflow position:

Eight ways of improving your cashflow

1. Before you give any credit, try to ensure your client is creditworthy.
2. Invoice your clients promptly to ensure fast payment.
3. Threaten overdue accounts with legal action. This will usually generate a response.
4. Try to discourage your clients from using your credit facility. Charge them a higher price for items bought on credit and offer a discount for goods settled on delivery or completion.
5. Keep your level of stock roughly in line with your sales.
6. Make a note of every phone call, quotation and estimate that you make and receive. You never know when this information may be needed.
7. Develop a very tight control over any credit that you give.
8. Always ask suppliers for credit for your business.

These points go part way to helping you manage your cashflow. Having money in the bank and keeping it there is really common sense. If you aim to get your clients to pay on time and delay the payment of your own suppliers then your financial position will improve. However, be careful not to get a reputation as a bad or slow payer: you may find your credit facilities severely reduced.

As your company prospers, you may well develop a cashflow problem with more and more overdue and unsettled invoices. You may then be able to turn to a factoring company to advance you up to 80 per cent of the value of these invoices. The balance will be payable when your clients settle their invoice less a handling charge for the original advance. (Factoring is covered in greater detail in Chapter 7.)

KEEPING BUSINESS ACCOUNTS

Regardless of the size of your business you are legally obliged to keep accurate and up-to-date financial records which detail all of your trading activities. There are many ways you can do this and it is not as complex as you might first think. In fact, the simpler the method you use the better. The system will then be easy to understand and maintain, and you can minimise the time spent doing your accounts and use it more productively building up your business.

Many people think a file full of receipts and invoices an adequate accounting system, but nothing could be further from the truth. These receipts and invoices have to be presented in such a way that you can clearly see what was purchased or sold and when.

- If your business is not registered for VAT then your accounting system can be very simple. All you need do is list your sales and receipts weekly or monthly, then subtract your business expenses from your total sales to give your profit or loss for the year.
- Even when your business becomes VAT registered your system does not have to become any more complex; you just need to keep a separate record for your VAT transactions. Your accountant will be able to advise you about the best method to use for your business.

Choosing your accounts system

Many different accounting systems are available. One of the best on the market is the **Simplex System** which is shown in Figure 8. This system is available from most good stationers, or direct from the publishers, George Vyner Limited, PO Box 1, Holmfirth HD9 7YP. Tel: 01484 685221. The *Simplex D Account Book* consists of 52 weekly pages as illustrated. Each page is ruled to take records of every activity likely to occur in a week, as listed below:

1. Receipts

This has a place to record cash, cheques and credit card vouchers taken on each day of the week. There is also a record for Other Receipts which include additional capital contributed by yourself, any loans received from the bank or finance house, refunds from the VAT office and so on.

Example No. 1 – Bank in Credit

Week No. 14 Commencing 2ND APRIL 200X

RECEIPTS

Day/Date	Daily Gross Takings: Cash Col 1	Cheques Col 2	Credit Cards Col 3	Other Receipts Col 4	Particulars
Sun : 2/4	186 27				
Mon : 3/4	232 44	25 80	19 95	35 60	TAX REFUND
Tues : 4/4	256 26			5 48	DEBTOR: P. SMITH
Wed : 5/4	112 27	12 64			
Thur : 6/4	289 85	19 74	41 05		
Fri : 7/4	364 24	26 34			
Sat : 8/4	382 72	62 50	72 95		
Sub Totals	1824 05	147 02	133 95	41 08	Total
Gross Weekly Takings (Cols 1 + 2 + 3)			2105 02		

PAID TO BANK

Cash Col 5	Cheques Col 6	Credit Cards Col 7	TOTAL Col 8
		19 95	19 95
420 00	66 88		486 88
440 00	58 72	41 05	539 77
860 00	125 60	61 00	1046 60

Totals

PAYMENTS FOR BUSINESS STOCK

Date or Chq. No.	To Whom Paid	Amount Paid By Cash Col 9	By Cheque Col 10
3/4	J. CONLAN & SONS	48 50	
659	J. BREWER & CO. LTD.		36 50
660	A.J. GOOD LTD.		136 85
5/4	J. BROWN & CO. LTD.	33 80	
7/4	F. LIVESEY & CO. LTD.	26 70	
661	A. NEWCOMBE		86 25
	Totals	109 00	259 60
	→		109 00
	Total payments (to Summary)		368 60

PAYMENTS OTHER THAN FOR STOCK

Nature of Payment	Amount Paid By Cash Col 11	By Cheque Col 12
Rent	35 00	
Rates		
Light and Heat		63 50
Carriage	9 45	
Postages £1·70; 24p; £2·38	4 32	
Paper		27 46
Motor Expenses PETROL	16 12	
-do- REPAIRS		86 50
Travelling	7 32	
Cleaning	5 00	
Printing & Stationery		23 20
Repairs & Renewals		15 78
Insurance (Business)		
Advertising		
Telephone		
Sundries	1 05	
Wages (Employees)	65 75	
Customs & Excise (VAT)		
Inland Revenue (Paye + NI)		27 96
Drawings of the Proprietor (see Note 4)	85 00	
Drawings – Partner 1		
Drawings – Partner 2		
Drawings – Partner 3		
Capital Items (see Note 3(1)).		
–do–		
Totals	229 01	244 40

WEEKLY BANK REPORT

Add	Opening Balance b/fwd from last week		1343 56
	Total Paid to bank during week (Col 8)		1046 60
	Start-up Allowance/Other Direct Credits		80 00
	Total		2470 16
Deduct	Cash drawn from bank	– –	
	Stock (Col 10) chqs only	259 60	
	Other payments (Col 12)	244 40	
	Standing Orders/Direct Debits	– –	
	Bank and Interest Charges	– –	
	Total		504 00
	Closing Balance carried forward		1966 16

WEEKLY CASH REPORT

Add	Cash in Hand (as counted) b/fwd from last week		6 46
	Gross Weekly Takings (Col 1 + Col 2 + Col 3)		2105 02
	Other Receipts (col 4)		41 08
	Cash Drawn from Bank		– –
	Total		2152 56
Deduct	Stock Payments (cash) (Col 9)	109 00	
	Other Payments (cash) (Col 11)	229 01	
	Amount paid to bank (Col 8)	1046 60	
	Total		1384 61
GEORGE VYNER LTD	Cash Balance on books		767 95
	Cash in hand (as counted) carr. fwd		767 60
	Difference on books (+ or –)	–	35

Fig. 8. The Simplex Weekly Page.

2. Paid to Bank

Records all amounts paid to the bank, whether cash, cheques or credit card vouchers, on any day of the week.

3. Payments for Business Stock

Here you can record all the purchases made by the business of stock for re-sale, or for raw materials to be made up into finished products.

4. Payments other than for stock

This is where you record all the expenses of your business which are not items for eventual re-sale. The various overheads have a line each. There is also room for such items as VAT and other payments to HM Revenue & Customs and drawings made by yourself or partners. Finally there is room to record any capital expenditure which represents the purchase of assets for long term use.

5. Weekly Cash Report

This will enable you to check the money received and paid in during the week and to discover any shortage or surplus. The special point to note here is that everything in your till – cash, cheques or credit card vouchers – is regarded as cash until it is finally paid into the bank, when, of course, it ceases to be 'cash in hand'.

6. Weekly Bank Report

This report will enable you to keep track of the balance that should be in your bank account at the end of each week. It consists of an opening balance at the start of the week, to which any sums paid into the bank are added (the total of column 8) and from which the sums paid by way of cheque are deducted. When you receive your bank statement you will be able to spot any direct credits received and any direct debits, standing orders or bank charges deducted. These can then be entered on the lines provided.

Each week the total takings, purchases, and expenses are carried to summaries at the back of the book. The figures from these summaries, when totalled for the year, enable you to compile your own final accounts and to discover the yearly profit or loss of your business. A fair copy of this final set of records can then be produced and submitted to the HMRC.

In addition to the *Simplex D Account Book*, George Vyner Ltd also produce a *Simplex Wages Book* and *VAT Record Book* designed to work in conjunction with the account book and complete the Simplex system. It is difficult to imagine a simpler set of book-keeping records. However, for those who do get into difficulty there is a free and confidential advice service and hot-line, available by contacting the Simplex Advice Bureau at George Vyner Limited.

Computerised book-keeping

If you have access to a computer then it may be worth considering using a computerised method of book-keeping which can be used to provide a clearer understanding of how your business is performing by:

- planning cashflow by identifying when bills need to be paid and when monies are due;
- managing VAT, tax and National Insurance payments;
- running an accurate payroll system;
- keeping accounts and up-to-date customer and supplier records;
- tracking credit card payments and recording cash sales;
- identifying consistent late payers to reduce the risk of bad debts;
- automatically managing and recording stock levels;
- reconciling your computerised accounts against your online bank accounts;
- producing annual accounts, end-of-year reports and monthly management reports, including profit and loss statements and balance sheets.

There are many different software packages to choose from but the best one for you will depend on the size and nature of your business. Popular programs include the following.

- *Pegasus Opera* – available from Pegasus Software Limited, Orion House, Orion Way, Kettering, Northamptonshire NN15 6PE. Tel: 01536 495000. Fax: 01536 495001. email: info@pegasus.co.uk Website: www.pegasus.co.uk
- *Sage Start-Up* and *Instant Accounts* – available from Sage (UK) Limited, North Park, Newcastle upon Tyne NE13 9AA. Tel: 0191 294 3000. Fax: 0845 2450295. Website: www.sage.co.uk
- *TAS Books* – available from TAS Softrware, North Park, Newcastle upon Tyne NE13 9AA. Tel: 0800 6940220. Fax: 0845 2450222. Email: sales@tassoftware co.uk Website: www.tassoftware.co.uk
- *Quickbooks Simple Start*, *Pro* and *Premier* – available from Intuit Limited, Statesman House, Stafferton Way, Maidenhead SL6 1AD. Tel: 0845 6062161. Email: uksales@intuit.com Website: http://quickbooks.intuit.co.uk

CHECKLIST

- Do you know how you will monitor the performance of your business?
- Are you aware of how to use your business plan after you have completed the document?
- Have you devised an effective method of managing your cashflow?
- Have you appointed an accountant to keep your books, or will you be doing this yourself?
- Have you selected an accountancy system to use?

CASE STUDIES

Joshua wants out

Running any business requires a tremendous amount of hard work, long hours and commitment. Unlike Jake, Joshua does not have a wife, children and a mortgage to support. He found the long hours and hard work put unbearable pressures on his social life and announced that he wished to sell his share of the business.

Unfortunately, Jake was not in a financial position to buy him out in order to retain complete control of the business. Instead he offered an investment opportunity to a member of his family to become a limited (sleeping) partner.

As with any partnership, it is important to choose your business partners well. It takes at least two to make any partnership a success but it only takes one to destroy it. Next time, Jake will be much more cautious.

Jasmine looks back

Looking back at all she had achieved from her humble beginnings in the spare bedroom of her home, Jasmine realised that if she had not taken the time to prepare a business plan in the first instance she would never have been as successful as she had become.

Even during the early days, Jasmine's business plan provided her with a clearly defined direction of where she was going and how she was going to get there. It made her realise the level of sales needed just to survive and how much more would be needed to succeed. She had realised that the only difference between surviving and succeeding is planning.

Regardless of whether you need any additional finance to launch your business it is still worth preparing a business plan to be sure in your own mind that you can succeed.

Luke finds a solution

With production and sales revenue increasing in line with his overdraft, Luke had to take drastic action if he was to avoid bankruptcy. He began by delegating many of his responsibilities to his key personnel, which gave him more time to concentrate on controlling his business.

His first task was to compile a set of management figures; had he done this a few months previously he could have avoided his present situation. These figures showed that if he were to use the services of a factoring company to exchange his outstanding invoices for cash, and then operate a strict credit control system, he would be able to pay off his overdraft and put his business back in a healthier condition.

Over some months this was done and Luke avoided certain bankruptcy. Now Luke always makes sure that he is never too busy to realise how his business is performing and is constantly monitoring his financial position.

Action points

1. Decide what methods you will use to monitor how well your business is performing and what steps will you take to overcome any loss of business.
2. Examine the various methods of book-keeping.
3. It is vital to keep a tight control over your cashflow. Which methods will you use to ensure your system is working?

Sample Business Plan

Phoenix Business Plans

Business Plan
200X

To: The Manager at The Euro Bank

From: Matthew Record

2A Grove Trading Estate, Dorcester, Dorset DT1 1ST
Telephone: 01305 269000 Fax: 01305 269001

CONTENTS

1. The Executive Summary

Phoenix Business Plans is a specialist fixed fee mail order service, launched to fill a niche that exists in the market place. We compile business plans rapidly and efficiently at a fraction of our competitors' prices, whilst maintaining the highest levels of quality and client satisfaction at all times. Our business is currently run by my wife and me.

We have kept our overheads to an absolute minimum in order to offer the client a service which is both extremely competitive and of the highest professional standards. Working from an office within our home we produce all of the business plans ourselves.

There are currently 450,000 new businesses starting up in Britain each year and whilst some will begin without the preparation of a business plan and succeed, the law of averages dictates otherwise. Some will prepare a plan on their own, or with the aid of the bank's forms, they will manage to a certain degree but the majority will use the services of a business such as ourselves. By offering a low cost, fixed fee service we believe this will give us the competitive edge and our business will be a huge success.

Our service will mainly be advertised in specialist business start up magazines and with the use of direct mailings. Clients will respond to these advertisements and word-of-mouth recommendations to order a business plan. An in-depth detailed questionnaire will then be despatched and it is from this information we will compile their business plans. Continuous telephone and fax support will be made available for an unlimited period of time should the client have any queries regarding any aspect of their plan.

It is our intention to remain a mail order company and solely supply the UK market for the foreseeable future. When we have established ourselves as a market leader and control a large market share, we will then look to promote our business on an international scale. In the meantime, we will welcome overseas orders should the situation ever occur.

We will need an initial investment of £1600 to get the business established; £1000 of this we have ourselves and the remaining £600 will be supplied with the aid of a business loan repayable over 24 months. To begin with, we conservatively estimate to receive one or two orders a week increasing to between three and five by the end of the first year. Our fixed fee service is £110.00 with additional copies of the business plans at £10.00 respectively. With these figures we expect to complete the first year of trading with a little over £14,000 in the bank.

2. The Nature of Our Business

2.1 Position to Date

All of our initial research has been fully compiled and as soon as we have purchased our computer system, printer and business stationery we will be in a position to commence trading.

2.2 Mission Statement

Phoenix Business Plans has been founded to fill a niche that exists in the market place. We will compile business plans rapidly and efficiently, at a fraction of our competitors' prices, whilst maintaining the highest levels of quality and client service at all times. The success of our business will be directly influenced by our dedication to continually improving the quality and service in every aspect of our operation.

2.3 Short Term Objectives

As a short term objective, it is our intention to launch our business in the most cost effective way in order to achieve the greatest market penetration. This will be achieved by beginning with a press release to all of the specialist business magazines and publications.

2.4 Long Term Objectives

When our business has become a fully established success we will be looking towards franchising the concept throughout the United Kingdom. As a franchised company we will have to be in a position to demonstrate a successful method of running and controlling the business which can be set up and run in any part of the country with equal success. This will be achieved by constantly monitoring and adapting our advertising and marketing methods in order to develop such a system.

2.5 Key Personnel

At present the business is run by my wife and myself. When we have established and maintained a larger market share and the work load outweighs our resources, we will then employ the use of outworkers to meet the demands of our clients.

2.6 Legal structure

Our business will be launched and trade under the name of Phoenix Business Plans. We will operate the business as a partnership between my wife, Helen Record and me, Matthew Record.

2.7 Professional advisers

We have appointed the services of Paul Whitehead as our solicitor for the business. He has already drawn up a partnership agreement and will be consulted as and when the situation arises. Until our sales revenue exceeds the VAT registration threshold our financial records will be kept with the aid of the Simplex accounting system and will be updated on a weekly basis by Helen Record.

3. Our Service

3.1 How Our Plans Are Produced

Each and every business plan will be compiled by me. I shall use a combination of a Windows-based Pentium computer, a Hewlett Packard Ink Jet Printer and special prestige ink jet paper. The finished document will be spiral bound and approximately 25 - 40 pages in length depending on how the client has responded to the questionnaire.

3.2 Our USP (Unique Selling Point)

Our main Unique Selling Point is the fact our service is operated on a fixed fee basis. Unlike accountants or management consultants who charge by the hour, our clients know in advance exactly how much our service will be and are then able to budget themselves accordingly. We believe this Unique Selling Point will provide us with a competitive edge which will ensure our business is successful.

3.3 Testing

A number of business plans have already been produced using the questionnaire system which has worked very well. As the questions are pre-set it is the clients who will spend their time researching the relevant information and not us. This means that we can accurately estimate the length of time it will take to compile a business plan and therefore we are able to offer a fixed fee service.

3.4 Sales Materials and Special Offers

An A5 sales leaflet will be produced and sent to prospects, business consultants, accountants *etc.* We will offer a 10 per cent discount to our clients if the plan is paid for in full at the time of ordering. A similar discount will be offered to business consultants *etc.* should their clients wish to order a plan through these organisations.

We have set ourselves a low profit margin in order to offer our clients value for money against the price of the competition. Therefore we have very little room to offer large discounts and as the average client is only likely to order a single business plan with a number of copies, then a bulk order will rarely occur. We strongly believe the high levels of service and client satisfaction that we provide will far outweigh any sales gimmick that we could offer.

3.5 Suppliers

As our business provides a service as opposed to manufacturing a product our main supplier will be Stanley Office Suppliers of Weymouth, Dorset. This company will be used to supply all of our stationery and office consumables.

4. The Market and the Competition

4.1 Our Target Market

The geographical area of our clientèle is only limited by the extent of our advertising and word-of-mouth recommendations. Our clients will mainly be private individuals who need to acquire additional capital to set up in business, as opposed to large firms seeking finance for expansion. However, that is not to say that we would be unable to meet their requirements should the situation ever arise.

Our target market also includes newly established businesses which should update their business plan periodically. This will enable those with capital invested in a business to see how well it is performing and enable the client to adapt to the changing needs of the business and its clients.

4.2 Market Positioning

We consider ourselves to be in the medium-price, medium-volume sector of the market place. By offering a fixed fee service we feel we will succeed against our competitors who charge an hourly rate and provide their clients with little indication as to how much their business plan will cost.

4.3 Quantity of Clients

To begin with we anticipate one or two clients a week which would increase to between three and five by the end of the first year. Each client will purchase at least one business plan and a number of copies. We will remain in contact with all our clients and will gently remind them when their business plan is due for renewal.

4.4 Client Response

Each time a client responds to an advertisement they will be sent an information pack which will contain full details about the service we offer, a very brief questionnaire, an application form and a return addressed envelope. The questionnaire will ask the client what they thought of the service that we offer and whether they will be using our services. The last section will ask them for any suggestions they may have about how we can improve upon the level of service we currently offer. We strongly believe the only way to survive in today's market place is to provide the client with the high level of client service and satisfaction they have come to expect and it is only by asking what they think of us that we are able to do this. It is important for us to listen to the needs of our clients; this will enable us to provide a level of service and client satisfaction that is second to none.

4.5 The Competition

A specialised business plan service is a niche market with huge growth potential, providing we are able to offer the right service to match the needs of our clients. The competition for this type of service is very minimal. Since researching the possibility of establishing such a service, I have only come across two direct competitors who offer a similar service. The first was in Bournemouth but their fee was just over 200 per cent more than ours. The second competitor was based in London and worked on an hourly rate; they were unable to estimate how much a plan would be. Both were contacted but neither contacted me again after I received their initial information.

4.6 Competition Price Comparison

Although our prices are approximately 200 per cent cheaper than that of our competitors, that does not mean the quality of our service is any less professional. As a company we promise to give our clients pure value for money and to do so have developed a service that will give us a medium profit margin with a high client turnover which we believe will be better than only a handful of clients with a high profit margin. We believe the more clients we have the sooner our name will become known in the market place and our market share will increase. Word-of-mouth recommendations are one of the most effective methods of advertising with the added benefit of it not costing anything. It is only by providing a professional service that we can achieve this.

5. The Marketing Plan

5.1 Anticipated Demand

The demand for the service we offer is determined by the level of new businesses starting up each year. At present this figure is estimated at some 450,000. The year before there was a 10 per cent fall in these figures. Low interest rates and the gradual rise of the economy have resulted in increased consumer spending thus putting confidence back into industry which in turn has the effect of more businesses starting up. It is estimated 200X will see a 15 per cent increase in the number of new businesses.

5.2 Marketing Methods

We will purchase a number of mailing lists and target 'Business Opportunity Seekers', for the time when they have found a business opportunity to suit them. If we target the right market then a good client list can be worth a lot more than it would cost to acquire.

We understand that advertising only reinforces, it does not generally sell. Therefore the information pack we send out will contain all the features and benefits of our business and marketing plans in order to convince the client to take the final step and order a plan. All inquiries will be followed up with a courtesy call a few days later to ensure the information pack has arrived and to ask whether we may be of any further assistance. National magazine advertisements will be placed on a monthly basis whilst the local press will be used on days of increased circulation.

5.3 Attracting Clients

We only have a small advertising budget at present so we will have to target our promotional methods effectively in order to produce the maximum response with the budget we have. To begin with, a press release will be sent to all local and national newspapers and specialist business magazines such as *Home Business*, *Enterprise*, *Business Franchise etc*. with details of the service we offer and where we can be contacted.

This will be followed up with direct mailings to potential clients who are in a position to use our services now. Business bankers, accountants, tax advisers *etc*. will also be approached, as these organisations deal directly on a daily basis with clients who are about to set up in business. Many of these organisations may be competing for our clients' business but we feel many of these will be too busy to undertake this type of work, whereas we are a specialist company dedicated to providing professionally packaged business plans. It is hoped that after a period of time most of our clients will be reached by word-of-mouth recommendations.

5.4 Public Relations

The service we provide will mainly help new small businesses which the press are keen to promote as the up-and-coming businesses of tomorrow. We will use the press to highlight our service as one which will help small businesses achieve long term success.

PHOENIX BUSINESS PLANS
1 JANUARY 200X TO

Month	**JAN**	**FEB**	**MAR**	**APR**	**MAY**	**JUN**
Sales	**440.00**	**660.00**	**880.00**	**880.00**	**1,100.00**	**1,100.00**
Materials	60.00	90.00	120.00	120.00	150.00	150.00
Labour	120.00	180.00	240.00	240.00	300.00	300.00
Cost of goods sold	**180.00**	**270.00**	**360.00**	**360.00**	**450.00**	**450.00**
Gross Profit	**260.00**	**390.00**	**520.00**	**520.00**	**650.00**	**650.00**
Overheads:						
Rent	0.00	0.00	0.00	0.00	0.00	0.00
Water Rates	4.00	4.00	4.00	4.00	4.00	4.00
Electricity & Gas	8.00	8.00	8.00	8.00	8.00	8.00
Postage & Carriage	12.00	18.00	24.00	24.00	30.00	30.00
Business Stationery	20.00	20.00	20.00	22.00	24.00	24.00
Repairs & Renewals	12.00	18.00	24.00	24.00	30.00	30.00
Insurance (Business)	10.00	10.00	10.00	10.00	10.00	10.00
Advertising	40.00	40.00	40.00	40.00	40.00	40.00
Telephone	20.00	20.00	20.00	20.00	20.00	20.00
Sundries	20.00	20.00	20.00	20.00	20.00	20.00
Professional Charges	0.00	50.00	0.00	0.00	0.00	0.00
Wages (Employees)	0.00	0.00	0.00	0.00	0.00	0.00
Bank & Interest Charges	0.00	0.00	0.00	0.00	0.00	0.00
National Insurance	22.50	22.50	22.50	22.50	22.50	22.50
Depreciation	26.00	26.00	26.00	26.00	26.00	26.00
Total Overheads	**194.50**	**256.50**	**218.50**	**220.50**	**234.50**	**234.50**
Net Profit	**65.50**	**133.50**	**301.50**	**299.50**	**415.50**	**415.50**
Interest Payable	3.50	3.50	3.50	3.50	3.50	3.50
Profit Before Tax	**62.00**	**130.00**	**298.00**	**296.00**	**412.00**	**412.00**
Taxation	15.50	32.50	74.50	74.00	103.00	103.00
Retained Profit	**46.50**	**97.50**	**223.50**	**222.00**	**309.00**	**309.00**

PROFIT & LOSS FORECAST
31 DECEMBER 200X

JLY	AUG	SEPT	OCT	NOV	DEC	Totals
1,650.00	**1,650.00**	**1,760.00**	**1,760.00**	**2,200.00**	**2,200.00**	**16,280.00**
225.00	225.00	240.00	240.00	300.00	300.00	2,220.00
450.00	450.00	480.00	480.00	600.00	600.00	4,440.00
675.00	**675.00**	**720.00**	**720.00**	**900.00**	**900.00**	**6,660.00**
975.00	**975.00**	**1,040.00**	**1,040.00**	**1,300.00**	**1,300.00**	**9,620.00**
0.00	0.00	0.00	0.00	0.00	0.00	0.00
4.00	4.00	4.00	4.00	4.00	4.00	48.00
8.00	8.00	8.00	8.00	8.00	8.00	96.00
45.00	45.00	48.00	48.00	60.00	60.00	444.00
30.00	30.00	36.00	36.00	42.00	42.00	346.00
45.00	45.00	48.00	48.00	60.00	60.00	444.00
10.00	10.00	10.00	10.00	10.00	10.00	120.00
40.00	40.00	40.00	40.00	40.00	40.00	480.00
20.00	20.00	20.00	20.00	20.00	20.00	240.00
20.00	20.00	20.00	20.00	20.00	20.00	240.00
0.00	0.00	0.00	0.00	0.00	0.00	50.00
0.00	0.00	0.00	0.00	0.00	0.00	0.00
0.00	0.00	0.00	0.00	0.00	0.00	0.00
22.50	22.50	22.50	22.50	22.50	22.50	270.00
26.00	26.00	26.00	26.00	26.00	26.00	312.00
270.50	**270.50**	**282.50**	**282.50**	**312.50**	**312.50**	**3,090.00**
704.50	**704.50**	**757.50**	**757.50**	**987.50**	**987.50**	**6,530.00**
3.50	3.50	3.50	3.50	3.50	3.50	42.00
701.00	**701.00**	**754.00**	**754.00**	**984.00**	**984.00**	**6,488.00**
175.25	175.25	188.50	188.50	246.00	246.00	1,622.00
525.75	**525.75**	**565.50**	**565.50**	**738.00**	**738.00**	**4,866.00**

6. The Operational Plan

6.1 Our Location

We are located in Dorchester, Dorset which is along the South Coast of England. As we are a mail order company then our location is irrelevant to the success of the business. To keep our overheads at an absolute minimum we work from home and will continue to do so in the short term. We have converted one of the rooms in our home into an office.

6.2 Client Support

Should our clients have any queries, then telephone support will be available throughout the completion of their business plan. We will only be too pleased to assist with anything from how to answer a particular question to whom the client should approach for finance. No charge will be made for this support and it is available to the client for an unlimited period of time.

6.3 Service Plan

All business plans need to be updated on a regular basis either bi-annually or preferably annually. We will maintain a client database and contact them shortly before their plan is due for renewal. After a client has used our services once, we aim to be able to provide them with our services for the duration of their business. As it is a service we provide, then after sales support is not an issue. However we will stay in contact with all our clients and hope they will use our services again.

6.4 Distribution Methods

As the geographical area of our target market is nationwide we will use Royal Mail for all our client correspondence. Our business and marketing plans are light documents so our carriage costs only represent a small percentage of turnover. We will guarantee the client a service to compile their business and marketing plans within 14 days following the receipt of the completed questionnaire. This is exactly half the delivery lead time quoted by our competitors.

6.5 Making The Sale

In an ideal world every enquiry would turn into a sale with the client completing the application form and returning it to us. However, as we do not live in an ideal world then we will have to work hard to achieve our sales targets. If after a week we have not had a response from a prospect, then a follow-up telephone call will be made to determine if the client is genuinely interested in our service. We estimate that for every three responses we get, one will develop into an order.

We will accept an initial 10 per cent deposit to compile a business plan. Then 50 per cent of the balance will be required when the questionnaire is returned and the remaining 40 per cent only when the client has received the plan and is completely satisfied with the service.

6.6 Samples

Sample business and marketing plans will be produced for members of the press as they request them. This will enable them to see exactly the service we offer and they will hopefully be able to include an appropriate article in their publication. Should they request it, clients will be sent sample pages of text so they can see the style and quality of our work.

6.7 Packaging

All business plans will contain a title page, contents page, main plan and financial details. These will be spiral bound and then despatched by first class post.

6.8 Job Responsibilities

As the manager I will produce each and every business plan myself. It is also my responsibility to actively promote the business and see to all aspects of its day-to-day running. My wife Helen is the proprietor and it is hoped that when our three young sons start school she will be able to take a more active role with the running of the business. At present Helen takes care of all the accounts and usually deals with all of the correspondence.

6.9 Insurance

We have discovered a very comprehensive home office insurance policy through our insurance broker, Connor Associates. The policy will be in force as from 9 December, 200X and will provide cover for the complete contents of our office including up to £2,000 in cash. We have also taken out an extra policy to provide cover against the increased cost of working due to business interruption. We have not taken out any public or employers' liability insurance as our clients use postal and telephone correspondence and at present we do not employ any staff members.

7. Financial Forecasts

7.1 Profit and loss forecast

See enclosed profit and loss forecast.

7.2 Profit and loss forecast explanatory notes

Sales – these figures assume an initial four clients during the first month of trading and then gradually increasing to 20 clients a month by the end of our first year. This will give us an estimated turnover of £16,280.00 in our first year.

Materials – paper, ink and binding are the only materials needed to compile a business plan. We have calculated these to be £15.00 for each 40 page document based on the price list supplied by Stanley Office Supplies. In order to meet our expected turnover, £2,220.00 of materials will be needed to produce our expected 148 business plans within the first year.

Labour – assuming each plan takes an average of six hours to compile, this estimate is equivalent to £5.00 per hour.

Cost of goods sold – it will cost £6,660.00 to produce sufficient business plans to meet our expected turnover of £16,280.00.

Gross profit – based on our enclosed figures we anticipate our annual gross profit will be £9,620.00.

Rent – as we intend to work from home, we will not incur any premises rental charges.

Water rates – we have allowed a 25 per cent contribution from the business towards the total cost of our residential water rates bill.

Electricity & gas – an additional 20 per cent has been added to our previous annual electricity and gas bills to allow for the extra use and then a 25 per cent contribution towards the new cost has been calculated.

PHOENIX BUSINESS PLANS
1 JANUARY 200X TO

Month	JAN	FEB	MAR	APR	MAY	JUN
Receipts						
Sales Receipts	440.00	660.00	880.00	880.00	1,100.00	1,100.00
Capital Introduced	1,000.00	0.00	0.00	0.00	0.00	0.00
Loans	600.00	0.00	0.00	0.00	0.00	0.00
Total Receipts	**2,040.00**	**660.00**	**880.00**	**880.00**	**1,100.00**	**1,100.00**
Payments:						
Materials	0.00	60.00	90.00	120.00	120.00	150.00
Salaries	120.00	180.00	240.00	240.00	300.00	300.00
Rent	0.00	0.00	0.00	0.00	0.00	0.00
Water Rates	4.00	4.00	4.00	4.00	4.00	4.00
Electricity & Gas	8.00	8.00	8.00	8.00	8.00	8.00
Postage & Carriage	12.00	18.00	24.00	24.00	30.00	30.00
Business Stationery	20.00	12.00	18.00	18.00	24.00	24.00
Repairs & Renewals	12.00	18.00	24.00	24.00	30.00	30.00
Insurance (Business)	10.00	10.00	10.00	10.00	10.00	10.00
Advertising	0.00	40.00	40.00	40.00	40.00	40.00
Telephone	20.00	20.00	20.00	20.00	20.00	20.00
Sundries	20.00	20.00	20.00	20.00	20.00	20.00
Capital items	750.00	0.00	0.00	0.00	0.00	0.00
Professional Charges	0.00	50.00	0.00	0.00	0.00	0.00
Wages (Employee's)	0.00	0.00	0.00	0.00	0.00	0.00
Customs & Excise (VAT)	0.00	0.00	0.00	0.00	0.00	0.00
National Insurance	0.00	22.50	22.50	22.50	22.50	22.50
Bank & Interest Charges	3.50	3.50	3.50	3.50	3.50	3.50
Loan Repayments	25.00	25.00	25.00	25.00	25.00	25.00
Total Payments	**1004.50**	**491.00**	**549.00**	**579.00**	**657.00**	**687.00**
Net Flow	1035.50	169.00	331.00	301.00	443.00	413.00
Opening Bank Balance	**0.00**	**1035.50**	**1204.50**	**1535.50**	**1836.50**	**2279.50**
Closing Bank Balance	**1035.50**	**1204.50**	**1535.50**	**1836.50**	**2279.50**	**2692.50**

CASHFLOW FORECAST
TO 31 DECEMBER 200X

JLY	AUG	SEPT	OCT	NOV	DEC	Total
1,650.00	1,650.00	1,760.00	1,760.00	2,200.00	2,200.00	16,280.00
0.00	0.00	0.00	0.00	0.00	0.00	1,000.00
0.00	0.00	0.00	0.00	0.00	0.00	600.00
1,650.00	**1,650.00**	**1,760.00**	**1,760.00**	**2,200.00**	**2,200.00**	**17,880.00**
150.00	225.00	225.00	240.00	240.00	300.00	1,920.00
450.00	450.00	480.00	480.00	600.00	600.00	4,440.00
0.00	0.00	0.00	0.00	0.00	0.00	0.00
4.00	4.00	4.00	4.00	4.00	4.00	48.00
8.00	8.00	8.00	8.00	8.00	8.00	96.00
45.00	45.00	48.00	48.00	60.00	60.00	444.00
30.00	30.00	36.00	36.00	42.00	42.00	332.00
45.00	45.00	48.00	48.00	60.00	60.00	444.00
10.00	10.00	10.00	10.00	10.00	10.00	120.00
40.00	40.00	40.00	40.00	40.00	40.00	440.00
20.00	20.00	20.00	20.00	20.00	20.00	240.00
20.00	20.00	20.00	20.00	20.00	20.00	240.00
0.00	0.00	0.00	0.00	0.00	0.00	750.00
0.00	0.00	0.00	0.00	0.00	0.00	50.00
0.00	0.00	0.00	0.00	0.00	0.00	0.00
0.00	0.00	0.00	0.00	0.00	0.00	0.00
22.50	22.50	22.50	22.50	22.50	22.50	247.50
3.50	3.50	3.50	3.50	3.50	3.50	42.00
25.00	25.00	25.00	25.00	25.00	25.00	300.00
873.00	**948.00**	**990.00**	**1005.00**	**1155.00**	**1215.00**	**10,153.50**
777.00	702.00	770.00	755.00	1045.00	985.00	7,726.50
2,692.50	**3,469.50**	**4,171.50**	**4,941.50**	**5,696.50**	**6,741.50**	**0.00**
3,469.50	**4,171.50**	**4,941.50**	**5,696.50**	**6,741.50**	**7,726.50**	**7,726.50**

Postage & carriage – each plan will cost £3.00 to despatch which includes a 20 per cent contribution towards the cost of sending information to potential clients who decide not to use our services.

Business stationery – this cost is based on the price list supplied by Stanley Office Supplies and includes letterheads, business cards, compliment slips and envelopes.

Repairs & renewals – a £4.00 contribution towards the costs of repairs and renewals has been calculated for each business plan sold.

Insurance (business) – the total annual cost of £120.00 has been estimated based on a home business insurance policy arranged through Connor Associates.

Advertising – this £40.00 monthly advertising cost is based on a £10.00 advertisement being placed in two monthly business magazines and the remaining £20.00 being used for classified advertising in local newspapers.

Telephone – an additional 20 per cent has been added to our previous annual telephone bill to allow for the extra use and then a 25 per cent contribution towards the new cost has been calculated.

Sundries – this cost is represented by tea, coffee, and various business magazines and newspapers.

Professional charges – this £50.00 cost is for our partnership agreement to be drawn up by our solicitor, Paul Whitehead.

Wages (employees) – we will not be in a position to employ anyone during our first year of trading.

Bank & interest charges – as we anticipate our account to be in credit we will take advantage of twelve months' free banking currently being offered by the bank.

National Insurance – our National Insurance contribution will be paid by monthly direct debit.

Depreciation – we anticipate our £500.00 second-hand computer system will be used in the business for two years before being replaced. This represents a monthly depreciation cost of £20.80. Our new printer will remain in use for four years which represents a monthly depreciation cost of £5.20.

Total overheads – our total overheads are estimated at £3,090.00.

Net profit – the above figures indicate that our expected net profit will be £6,530.00.

Interest payable – assuming the bank will advance us £600.00 at 12.9 per cent APR this represents a total monthly repayment charge of £28.50 of which £3.50 is interest.

Profit before tax – our annual profit before tax is calculated at £6,488.00.

Taxation – this total cost of £1,622.00 is calculated at 25 per cent of the profit made by the business.

Retained profit – using the enclosed figures we should complete our first year of trading with a retained profit of £4,866.00.

7.3 Cashflow forecast

See enclosed cashflow forecast.

7.4 Cashflow forecast explanatory notes

Sales Receipts – *see profit and loss forecast.*

Capital Introduced – this £1,000.00 represents our initial investment taken from our personal savings which will remain in the business for the duration of our trading life.

Loans – this figure of £600.00 represents the two year loan we expect to obtain from the bank.

Total receipts – this figure of £17,880.00 is calculated by totalling our sales receipts (£16,280.00), capital introduced (£1000.00) and loans (£600.00).

Materials – *see profit and loss forecast.*

Salaries – as we will only draw a salary from the business plans actually sold this figure of £4,440.00 is based on the total plans sold during our first year. Although this does not represent a large amount of money, by December we anticipate compiling at least 20 business plans a month which will give us an income of at least £600.00 per month.

Rent – *see profit and loss forecast.*

Water rates – *see profit and loss forecast.*

Electricity & gas – *see profit and loss forecast.*

Postage & carriage – *see profit and loss forecast.*

Business stationery – *see profit and loss forecast.*

Repairs & renewals – *see profit and loss forecast.*

Insurance (business) - *see profit and loss forecast.*

Advertising – *see profit and loss forecast.*

Telephone – *see profit and loss forecast.*

Sundries – *see profit and loss forecast.*

Capital items – the total cost of £750.00 comprises a second-user computer system at £500.00 and a new inkjet printer at £250.00 which we will need to purchase at the end of December 200X.

Professional charges – *see profit and loss forecast.*

Wages (employees) – *see profit and loss forecast.*

Customs & Excise (VAT) – as our expected annual turnover of £16,280.00 is below the £64,000.00 registration limit we will not be registered for VAT during our first year of trading.

National Insurance – *see profit and loss forecast.*

Bank & interest charges – with free banking for the first year our only interest charges will be £42.00 which represents the interest payable on our £600.00 loan from the bank.

Loan repayments – borrowing £600.00 over two years with 12.9 per cent interest represents a annual repayment of £300.00.

Total payments – we expect our total payments for the first year to be £10,153.50.

Net flow – even though our net flow indicates steady financial growth, we will still require a £600.00 loan as a contingency in the event our sales receipts do not meet our expectations or our payments exceed our estimates.

PHOENIX BUSINESS PLANS
1 JANUARY 200X

Month	**JAN**	**FEB**	**MAR**	**APR**	**MAY**	**JUN**
Fixed Assets	**724.00**	**698.00**	**672.00**	**646.00**	**620.00**	**594.00**
Current Assets						
Raw Materials	0.00	0.00	0.00	0.00	0.00	0.00
Debtors	0.00	0.00	0.00	0.00	0.00	0.00
Cash in the Bank	1,035.50	1,204.50	1,535.50	1,836.50	2,279.50	2,692.50
Total Current Assets	**1,035.50**	**1,204.50**	**1,535.50**	**1,836.50**	**2,279.50**	**2,692.50**
Current Liabilities						
Creditors	122.50	160.50	192.50	196.50	226.50	226.50
Tax Liability	15.50	48.00	122.50	196.50	299.50	402.50
Overdraft	0.00	0.00	0.00	0.00	0.00	0.00
Total Liabilities	**138.00**	**208.50**	**315.00**	**393.00**	**526.00**	**629.00**
Net Current Assets	**897.50**	**996.00**	**1,220.50**	**1,443.50**	**1,753.50**	**2,063.50**
Net Assets	**1,621.50**	**1,694.00**	**1,892.50**	**2,089.50**	**2,373.50**	**2,657.50**
Financed by:						
Capital introduced	1000.00	1000.00	1000.00	1000.00	1000.00	1000.00
Bank Loans	575.00	550.00	525.00	500.00	475.00	450.00
Retained Profit	46.50	144.00	367.50	589.50	898.50	1,207.50
Total Capital	**1,621.50**	**1,694.00**	**1,892.50**	**2,089.50**	**2,373.50**	**2,657.50**

BALANCE SHEET FORECAST TO 31 DECEMBER 200X

JLY	AUG	SEPT	OCT	NOV	DEC
568.00	**542.00**	**516.00**	**490.00**	**464.00**	**438.00**
0.00	0.00	0.0	0.00	0.00	0.00
0.00	0.00	0.0	0.00	0.00	0.00
3,469.50	4,171.50	4,941.50	5,696.50	6,741.50	7,726.50
3,469.50	**4,171.50**	**4,941.50**	**5,696.50**	**6,741.50**	**7,726.50**
301.50	301.50	316.50	316.50	376.50	376.50
577.75	753.00	941.50	1,130.00	1,376.00	1,622.00
0.00	0.00	0.0	0.00	0.00	0.00
879.25	**1,054.50**	**1,258.00**	**1,446.50**	**1,752.50**	**1,998.50**
2,590.25	**3,117.00**	**3,683.50**	**4,250.00**	**4,989.00**	**5,728.00**
3,158.25	**3,659.00**	**4,199.50**	**4,740.00**	**5,453.00**	**6,166.00**
1,000.00	1,000.00	1,000.00	1,000.00	1,000.00	1,000.00
425.00	400.00	375.00	350.00	325.00	300.00
1,733.25	2,259.00	2,824.50	3,390.00	4,128.00	4,866.00
3,158.25	**3,659.00**	**4,199.50**	**4,740.00**	**5,453.00**	**6,166.00**

Opening bank balance – this figure simply represents the closing balance from the preceding month of trading.

Closing bank balance – we anticipate completing our first year of trading with a closing bank balance of £7,726.50.

7.5 Balance sheet forecast

See enclosed forecast.

7.6 Balance sheet explanatory notes

Fixed assets – these include our second-user computer system and our new inkjet printer. The net worth of these assets has been calculated in accordance with the depreciation described in the *Profit and loss explanatory notes.*

Current assets

Raw materials – as we offer a service as opposed to manufacturing a product, we will not carry any raw materials in stock.

Debtors – as our clients will pay for their business plans in full before being despatched, we will not have any debtors.

Cash in the bank – the amount of money we will have in the bank at any given time is illustrated in our cashflow forecast.

Total current assets – as we neither carry raw materials nor have any debtors our total current assets are represented solely by the cash we have in the bank.

Current liabilities

Creditors – we anticipate keeping our creditors to an absolute minimum but we will take advantage of credit given by companies providing items such as materials, business stationery, insurance and advertising. Our National Insurance payments are also listed under creditors as they will be paid monthly in arrears.

Tax liability – this is calculated from the tax due on our business profits as illustrated in the profit and loss forecast.

Overdraft – providing we meet our sales projections and we do not exceed our expected payments, then we do not anticipate the need for an overdraft facility.

Total liabilities – as we will not have an overdraft, our total liabilities will be represented by the total of our creditors and tax liability which we estimate to be £1,998.50.

Net current assets – we have calculated the difference between our *Total current assets* and our *Total liabilities* to be £5,728.00 at our year end.

Financed by

Capital introduced – this will remain at £1,000.00; see our cashflow forecast for further information.

Bank loans – having repaid £300.00 of our £600.00 loan at £25.00 per month during our first year of trading, we will be left with the balance of £300.00 remaining at the end of our first year.

Retained profit – this will be £4,866.00; see our profit and loss forecast for further information.

Total capital – at the end of our first year of trading we anticipate having accumulated £6,166.00 in total capital/net assets.

8. Financial Requirements

8.1 Required Finance

Our business will require a capital investment of £1600.00 to get established. We have £1000.00 ourselves and require an additional bank loan of £600.00. All funds will need to be in place by 15 December 200X. This will enable us to purchase the computer, printer, software and stationery prior to the launch of the business on 9 January 200X.

8.2 Risks

If this country was ever unfortunate enough to suffer another recession then obviously the amount of new businesses starting up would decrease, as would our initial target market. Even in times of recession, new businesses will be set up and the demand for a low cost, quality service such as ours would probably improve as clients use their budgets more wisely. However, if this was not the case, then being a resourceful company we would diversify our market and target those businesses already trading to make them see the key to success is careful business planning which our service provides. As we are primarily a mail order company then a postal strike will have a detrimental effect on our business. This would be overcome by using parcel couriers. Our carriage costs would rise quite considerably for the duration of the strike but we would still be providing the client with a level of service that is second to none.

Glossary

Accounts. A set of financial statements detailing the financial transactions of a business.

Advertising. Use of paid media to publicise a business in order to persuade clients to buy.

Analysis. The separation of an item into sections to enable it to be examined and described.

Assets. Items or property with monetary values which are owned by a business or individual.

Assumptions. Estimates made concerning future developments which cannot be supported with facts.

Balance sheet. A statement illustrating the financial position of a business at any given time.

Break-even point. The point at which the total sales revenue is equal to the total costs.

Budget. A financial estimate of future revenue and expenditure.

Business objectives. The goals set by a business which they hope to be able to achieve.

Business plan. A detailed statement describing the nature of a business – its trading details, business objectives and competitors, including financial forecasts detailing current and future requirements.

Business partnership. The legal trading of two or more individuals trading together as a business in accordance with the Partnership Act (1890).

Capital. A combination of both long-term funds and assets which are either owned by or loaned to a business.

Capital gains tax. The tax due to HMRC on any profit produced by the sale of an asset.

Cashflow forecast. A financial forecast which estimates actual cash payments coming into and going out of a business, for example each month.

Contract (written). A document listing the rules and conditions of an agreement between two or more parties.

Creditors. Businesses or individuals to which you owe money for work they have done or materials they have supplied.

Current assets. Assets which are either cash or can realistically be exchanged for cash within a 12-month period, *eg* stock, work in progress, and debtors.

Current liabilities. Short term debts which must be repaid within a 12-month period, including bank overdrafts.

Debtors. Businesses or individuals by whom the business is owed money for work done or materials supplied.

Depreciation. The decline in value of assets during the course of their working life.

Desk research. A source of obtaining information directly from already published materials.

Direct mail. A method used to directly target existing or potential clients with information about goods or services offered by a business.

Distribution. Methods by which organisations transport their products to their clients.

Exhibitions. A way of displaying and demonstrating your products or services to a large number of potential or existing clients at a particular venue.

Factoring. A service offered by certain businesses to exchange unpaid invoices for cash.

Field research. A source of obtaining various information directly from the general public through a combination of surveys and questionnaires.

Finance lease. A lease in which the lessee (user) will be given the opportunity to purchase the leased item when the lease expires.

Fixed assets. Long-term assets which will be retained and used by a business as opposed to being quickly resold. Typical examples are land, buildings, plant, machinery and vehicles.

Fixed costs. The costs which will remain constant regardless of any change to the level of business. Typical examples include rent, rates and depreciation.

Franchise. A business whereby the owner (franchisor) grants the user (franchisee) a licence to trade under the brand name of the franchisor in exchange for a royalty.

Grants. Money awarded by the government and/or local authorities for specific purposes such as urban regeneration or development in rural areas.

Hire purchase. A method used to purchase goods over an extended period of time using a credit facility and then making regular fixed repayments.

Insurance. A way of compensating a business or individual for any loss.

Investment. A commitment made by an organisation to increase the financial or physical assets of a business; for example, in the form of plant, machinery or equipment.

Limited company. An organisation in which a number of people invest capital in return for a share of ownership of the company.

Limited liability. The maximum loss for which a shareholder is personally liable; the amount of capital which they have agreed to invest (*ie* pay for their shares).

Loan. An advance of a specified sum of money by a lender which is repayable, usually with interest, over a specified period of time by the borrower.

Market research. A method of investigation used to determine the nature of a particular market and to ascertain current market trends.

Marketing. A process used to identify client requirements and then supply appropriate products or services to satisfy those needs.

Marketing mix. A combination of various marketing methods used to generate sales. The methods may include advertising, pricing and sales promotions.

Overdraft. A facility provided by a financial institution to allow the borrower to withdraw money from their account up to a pre-set amount.

Patent. An ownership right granted by the government to the inventor of an entirely new product or manufacturing process.

Private limited company. A company which only issues shares to private individuals.

Product life cycle. A sales pattern showing the rise of a product from the initial launch through to its eventual decline.

Profit and loss account. A financial summary illustrating the sales revenue of a business and of all the costs incurred to obtain this revenue.

Public limited company. A company which issues shares to the general public through the Stock Exchange.

Sales revenue. The income generated by a business following the sale of its goods or services.

Sensitivity analysis. A method used to determine how the results of a financial analysis will be affected following a change made to any of the assumptions.

Sole trader. A business owned and operated by a private individual.

Stock. The name given to finished products which are owned by a business and ready for sale, and to raw materials to produce these products.

Turnover. The total amount of revenue which has been generated directly from sales.

Unlimited liability. The owners of a business with unlimited liability status are personally liable for any debts incurred by the business. This includes sole traders and most partnerships.

Variable costs. Costs, such as raw material costs, which will vary directly according to the level of output.

VAT. (Valued Added Tax) Government-imposed indirect taxation charged on products and services at a set rate.

Work in progress. Goods which are in the process of being completed.

Working capital. Readily available money used to finance the day-to-day running of a business.

Useful Addresses

ACCOUNTING

Asset Based Finance Association (ABFA), Boston House, The Little Green, Richmond, Surrey TW9 1QE. Tel: 020 8332 9955. Fax: 020 8332 2585. Website: www.abfa.org.uk

Association of Chartered Certified Accountants (ACCA), 29 Lincoln's Inn Fields, London WC2A 3EE. Tel: 020 7059 5000. Fax: 020 7059 5050. Email: info@accaglobal.com Website: www.accaglobal.com

George Vyner Limited, PO Box 1, Holmfirth HD9 7YP. Tel: 01484 685221. Suppliers of the *Simplex* accounting systems.

The Institute of Chartered Accountants in England and Wales (ICAEW), Chartered Accountants' Hall, PO Box 433, London EC2P 2BJ. Tel: 020 7920 8100. Fax: 020 7920 0547. Email: psogen@icaew.com Website: www.icaew.co.uk

The Institute of Chartered Accountants of Scotland (ICAS), CA House, 21 Haymarket Yards, Edinburgh EH12 5BH. Tel: 0131 347 0100. Fax: 0131 347 0105. Email: enquiries@icas.org.uk Website: www.icas.org.uk

Intuit Limited, Statesman House, Stafferton Way, Maidenhead SL6 1AD. Tel: 0845 6062161. Email: uksales@intuit.com Website: http://quickbooks.intuit.co.uk Suppliers of *Quick Books* accountancy software.

Pegasus Software Limited, Orion House, Orion Way, Kettering, Northamptonshire NN15 6PE. Tel: 01536 495000. Fax: 01536 495001. Email: info@:pegasus.co.uk Website: www.pegasus.co.uk Suppliers of accountancy software.

Sage (UK) Limited, North Park, Newcastle upon Tyne NE13 9AA. Tel: 0191 294 3000. Fax: 0845 2450295. Website: www.sage.co.uk
Suppliers of accountancy software

TAS Software, North Park, Newcastle upon Tyne NE13 9AA. Tel: 0800 6940220. Fax: 0845 2450222. Email: sales@tassoftware.co.uk
Website: www.tassoftware.co.uk
Suppliers of accountancy software.

BUSINESS PLAN PREPARATION

PlanIT Business Plan Deluxe – avialable from A World of Software, The Harlequin Centre, Watford WD17 2UB. Tel: 01923 630259.
Email: orders@aworldofsoftware.com
Website: www.aworldofsoftware.com

Business Planner – available from Rosetta IT Solutions Limited. Tel: 01942 814814. Email: support@rosetta-it.com
Website: www.rosetta-it.com

Business Plan Pro – available from PaloAlto Software Limited, 72 Hammersmith Road, London W14 8TH. Tel: 0845 351 9924.
Fax: 020 7900 2773. Email: sales@paloalto.co.uk
Websites: www.businessplanpro.co.uk or www.paloalto.co.uk

FINANCIAL

Alliance & Leicester plc, Carlton Park, Narborough, Leicester LE19 0AL. Tel: 0116 201 1000. Fax: 0116 200 4040.
Website: www.alliance-leicester-group.co.uk

Barclays Bank. Website: www.barclays.com

British Insurance Brokers' Association (BIBA), 14 Bevis Marks, London EC3A 7NT. Tel: 0901 8140015. Fax: 020 7626 9676. Email: enquiries@biba.org.uk
Website: www.biba.org.uk

British Private Equity and Venture Capital Association (BVCA), 3 Clements Inn, London WC2A 2AZ. Tel: 020 7025 2950. Fax: 020 7025 2951.
Email: bvca@bvca.co.uk Website: www.bvca.co.uk

Close Invoice Finance, Southbrook House, 25 Bartholomew Street, Newbury, Berkshire RG14 5LL. Tel: 01635 508 400. Fax: 01635 521 180.
Email: info@closeinvoice.co.uk Website: www.closeinvoice.co.uk

Co-operative Bank, PO Box 101, 1 Balloon Street, Manchester M60 4EP. Tel: 08457 212 212. Website: www.co-operativebank.co.uk

Enterprise Investments Scheme (EIS), Erico House, 93–99 Upper Richmond Road, London SW15 2TG. Tel: 020 8785 5560. Fax: 020 8785 5561. Email: members@eisa.org.uk Website: www.eisa.org.uk

Financial Ombudsman Service, South Quay Plaza, 183 Marsh Wall, London E14 9SR. Tel: 020 7964 1000. Fax: 020 7964 1001. Website: www.financial-ombudsman.org.uk

HSBC, 8 Canada Square, London E14 5HQ. Tel: 020 7991 8888. Website: www.hsbc.com

Independent Banking Advisory Service (IBAS), Somersham, Huntingdon PE28 3WD. Tel: 01487 843444. Fax: 01487 740607. Email: help@ibas.co.uk Website: www.ibas.co.uk

Lloyds TSB Bank plc, 25 Gresham Street, London EC2V 7HN. Tel: 01444 459 144. Website: www.lloydstsb.com

NatWest Bank plc, 135 Bishopsgate, London EC2M 3UR. Tel: 0800 200 400. Website: www.natwest.com

The Prince's Trust, 18 Park Square East, London NW1 4LH. Tel: 020 7543 1234. Fax: 020 7543 1200. Email: webinfops@princes-trust.org.uk Website: www.princes-trust.org.uk

Royal Bank of Scotland plc. Registered office: 36 St Andrew Square, Edinburgh EH2 2YB. Website: www.rbs.com

Small Firms Loan Guarantee, Department for Business, Enterprise & Regulatory Reform (BERR), 1 Victoria Stret, London SW1H 0ET. Tel: 020 7215 5000. Fax: 020 7215 01015. Email: enquiries@berr.gsi.gov.uk Website: www.berr.gov.uk

GENERAL BUSINESS HELP

The British Chambers of Commerce, 65 Petty France, London SW1H 9EU. Tel: 020 7654 5800. Fax: 020 7654 5819. Email: info@britishchambers.org.uk Website: www.britishchambers.org.uk

Business in the Community, 137 Shepherdess Walk, London N1 7RQ. Tel: 020 7566 8650. Email: information@bitc.org.uk Website: www.bitc.org.uk

Business Link. Tel: 0845 600 9 006. Website: www.businesslink.gov.uk

Federation of Small Businesses, Sir Frank Whittle Way, Blackpool Business Park, Blackpool FY4 2FE.
Tel: 01253 336000. Fax: 01253 348046. Email: ho@fsb.org.uk
Website: www.fsb.org.uk

National Federation Self Employed and Small Businesses Ltd, 114 Barnby Gate, Newark, Nottinghamshire NG24 1QR. Tel: 01636 610417.
Fax: 01522 511423.

Small Business Bureau Limited, Curzon House, Church Road, Windlesham, Surrey GU20 6BH. Tel: 01276 452010. Fax: 01276 451602.
Email: info@sbb.org.uk Website: www.smallbusinessbureau.org.uk

TACK International, TACK House, Latimer Park, Chesham, Buckinghamshire HP5 1TR. Tel: 01494 766633. Fax: 01494 766622. Email@ info@tack.co.uk
Website: www.tackco.uk

LEGAL

The Chartered Institute of Patent Attorneys, 95 Chancery Lane, London WC2A 1DT. Tel: 020 7405 9450. Fax: 020 7430 0471.
Email: mail@cipa.org.uk Website: www.cipa.org.uk

Companies House, Crown Way, Maindy, Cardiff CF14 3UZ. Tel: 0870 333 3636. Email: enquiries@companies-house.gov.uk
Website: www.companieshouse.gov.uk

Consumer Direct. Tel: 08454 04 05 06. Website: www.consumerdirect.gov.uk

Health and Safety Executive (HSE), Caerphilly Business Park, Caerphilly CF83 3GG. Tel: 0845 345 0055 (Infoline). Fax: 08454 089 566.
Email: hse.infoline@natbrit.com Website: www.hse.gov.uk

HM Revenue and Customs (HMRC). Website: www.hmrc.gov.uk

Information Commissioner's Office (ICO), Wycliffe House, Water Lane, Wilmslow, Chesire SK9 5AF. Tel: 01625 545700. Fax: 01625 524 510.
Email: mail@ico.gsi.gov.uk Website: www.ico.gov.uk

The Institute of Patentees and Inventors, PO Box 39296, London SE3 7WH.
Tel: 0871 226 2091. Fax: 020 8293 5920. Email@ ipi@invent.org.uk
Website: www.invent.org.uk

Institute of Trade Mark Attorneys, Canterbury House, 2–6 Sydenham Road, Croydon, Surrey CR0 9XE. Tel: 020 8686 2052. Fax: 020 8680 5723.
Email: tm@itma.org.uk Website: www.itma.org.uk

The Law Society, 113 Chancery Lane, London WC2A 1PL. Tel: 020 7242 1222. Fax: 020 7831 0344. Website: www.lawsociety.org.uk

Office of Fair Trading (OFT), Fleetbank House, 2–6 Salisbury Square, London EC4Y 8JX. Tel: 08457 22 44 99. Website: www.oft.gov.uk

Pensions Advisory Service, 11 Belgrave Road, London SW1V 1RB. Tel: 0845 6012923. Fax: 020 7233 8016. Email: enquiries@pensionsadvisoryservice.org.uk Website: www.pensionsadvisoryservice.org.uk

UK Intellectual Property Office (IPO), Concept House, Cardiff Road, Newport NP10 8QQ. Tel: 0845 9500505. Email: enquiries@ipo.gov.uk Website: www.ipo.gov.uk

MARKETING AND ADVERTISING

Amber Promotions, Alpha 319, Chobham Business Centre, Chertsey Road, Chobham GU24 8JB. Tel: 0845 370 3800. Email: sales@amberpromotions.co.uk Website: www.promotional-items-gifts-co.uk

Chartered Institute of Marketing (CIM), Moor Hall, Cookham, Maidenhead, Berkshire SL6 9QH. Tel: 01628 427500. Fax: 01628 427499. Email: info@cim.co.uk Website: www.cim.co.uk

Committee of Advertising Practice (CAP), Mid City Place, 71 High Holborn, London WC1V 6QT. Tel: 020 7492 2222. Fax: 020 7242 3696. Email: enquiries@cap.org.uk Website: www.cap.org.uk

Direct Selling Association (DSA), 29 Floral Street, London WC2E 9DP. Tel: 020 7497 1234. Fax: 020 7497 3144. Email: info@dsa.org.uk Website: www.dsa.org.uk

The Institute of Direct Marketing (IDM), 1 Park Road, Teddington, Middlesex TW11 0AR. Tel: 020 8614 0277. Fax: 020 8943 2535. Email: enquiries@theidm.com Website: www.theidm.com

Mail Preference Service (MPS), FREEPOST 29 LON20771, London W1E 0ZT. Tel: 0845 703 4599. Fax: 020 7323 4226. Email: mps@dma.org.uk Website: www.mpsonline.org.uk

The Market Research Society (MRS), 15 Northburgh Street, London EC1V 0AH. Tel: 020 7490 4911. Fax: 020 7490 0608. Email: info@mrs.org.uk Website: www.mrs.org.uk

The Marketing Society, 1 Park Road, Teddington, Middlesex TW11 0AR. Tel: 020 8973 1700. Fax: 020 8973 1701. Website: www.marketing-society.org.uk

Nobo Visual Aids Limited, Alder Close, Compton Industrial Estate, Eastbourne, Sussex BN23 6QB. Tel: 01323 641521.

Office for National Statistics, Cardiff Road, Newport NP10 8XG. Tel: 0845 601 3034. Fax: 01633 652747. Email: info@statistics.gov.uk Website: www.statistics.gov.uk

Pinewood Associates, Hardy Street, Manchester M30 7NN. Tel: 0161 7076000. Fax: 0161 7076766. email@ sales@pinewoodassociates.com Website: www.pinewoodassociates.com

Royal Mail. Website: www.royalmail.com

YOUR BUSINESS IDEA

Association of Event Organisers Limited, 119 High Street, Berkhamsted, Hertfordshire HP4 2DJ. Tel: 01442 285810. Fax: 01442 875551. Email: info@aeo.org.uk Website: www.aeo.org.uk

British Franchise Association, A2 Danebrook Court, Oxford Office Village, Langford Lane, Oxford OX5 1LQ. Tel: 01865 379892. Fax: 01865 379 946. Website: www.thebfa.org

BSI British Standards, 389 Chiswick High Road, London W4 4AL. Tel: 020 8996 9001. Fax: 020 8996 7001. Email: cservices@bsigroup.com Website: www.bsi-global.com

Department for Business, Enterprise & Regulatory Reform (BERR), 1 Victoria Street, London SW1H 0ET. Tel: 020 7215 5000. Fax: 020 7215 0105. Email: enquiries@berr.gsi.gov.uk Website: www.berr.gov.uk

Exhibitions and Trade Fairs. Website: www.exhibitions.co.uk

Other Small Business books from How To Books

85 Inspiring Ways to Market Your Small Business, Jackie Jarvis
Book-Keeping & Accounting for the Small Business, Peter Taylor
Employing Staff in the Small Business, Antonia Barber and Susan Mcgaughran
How to Get Free Publicity, Pam and Bob Austin
How to Grow Your Small Business Rapidly *Online,* Jim Green
How to Turn Your Business into the Next Global Brand, Brian Duckett and Paul Monaghan
Marketing for the Micro-Business, Jack Roberts
Mastering Book-Keeping, Dr Peter Marshall
Prepare to Sell Your Company, L B Buckingham
Raising Finance for Your Business, Mark Blayney
Setting Up & Running a Limited Company, Robert Browning
Starting Your Own Business, Jim Green
The Small Business Start-Up Workbook, Cheryl D Rickman

Index